Dig Under or Crawl Over

An Album of Memories

Dig Under or Crawl Over

An Album of Memories

written by
Vivian Baird McLennan

compiled and edited by
Mary Nelle McLennan
and
Richard L. Welsh

Dig Under or Crawl Over
An Album of Memories

written by
Vivian Baird McLennan

compiled and edited by
Mary Nelle McLennan and Richard L. Welsh

© 2021

Published by Wise & Spry Publishing (Marie J Amerson)
PO Box 26364
Macon, Georgia 31221

ISBN - 978-0-9894116-7-7

"THERE IS NO BETTER WAY TO GET TO KNOW SOMEONE THAN
TO LISTEN—REALLY LISTEN—TO THEIR STORIES."

Vivian Baird McLennan

◆————————————————◆

Dedication

*This combined work of heart
is dedicated to our world's storytellers
and to all who really listen.*

CONTENTS

Contents

Part Three
Life in Brighton as We Knew It

Part Four
Foolishness and Fun

Contents

How This Came to Be

It didn't start out to be a book. This album of memories actually began as a practical way to keep my ninety-year-old mother, Vivian Baird McLennan, busy and out of trouble while spending long winters with my husband Rick Welsh and me in cold Pittsburgh, Pennsylvania.

Vivian, never having been one who "sat well," was bored being away from her Brighton, Tennessee, home. Living seven hundred fifty miles and months away from her life-long community was tough for her. She missed the usual projects she dabbled in—futzing around in her yard; stripping and refinishing furniture; endlessly reorganizing her cache of memorabilia; and spending Fridays with folks at The Hub, Clopton's charity store. Even pampering two grand-dogs, helping with daily chores, listening to Talking Books from the Library of Congress, and watching the History Channel back when it really was about history were just not enough. She needed a project!

To keep "Memmie" interested and engaged during her months away from home, we encouraged her to put into writing the multitude of vivid memories she'd shared through her storytelling over the years. It took a bit of prompting, but soon she was hooked.

Rick and I turned one of our guest rooms into an office for her, a writer's den of sorts. We supplied her with dozens of dark felt-tipped pens, reams of bold-lined paper, and a couple of bright task lamps to accommodate her vision loss due to macular degeneration. She routinely had to use her prescribed magnifying aids to read even her own writing. Oddly, she asked for a bag of rubber bands, which was an easy dollar store purchase, although I still don't quite know how she used so many of them. Then she took it from there.

Most days, after joining us for breakfast, "Mem" would retreat to her office and lose herself in the past, painstakingly hand-scribing a memory in her bold, increasingly shaky handwriting. She wrote each story by hand numerous times, starting over from scratch and editing until she captured its essence on paper. She usually came down for lunch, but soon returned to her writing or perhaps to steal a nap. Around 4:00 each afternoon, she again joined us downstairs and shared her day's work.

The following account shows how those winter afternoons usually unfolded:

> "You ready for some Tennessee tales?" she routinely chimed after thumping down the stairs, warily placing one foot, then the other, on each step for security. She clutched a batch of bold-lined sheets of paper saturated with darkly scribed cursive. At the bottom of the stairs, she reached for her cherry-red Rolator and began her slow cruise toward the toasty family room.

"Sure, Mem! Whatcha' got for us today?" came Ricks' usual response to her cheerful "call to order." Nestled in his recliner, he cradled his open laptop and prepared for another story session.

Snow drifted against the French doors more days than not. Winds whipped holly branches against the porch uprights, but the fireplace glow added a warm welcome for my ninety-two-year-old mother and whatever she was bringing with her that day. She rolled her way toward her usual perch on the loveseat, then, scoot by scoot, inched herself around until she could leave the safety of the Rolator and plop into place. Finally, she raised the footrest so she could stretch out her abbreviated 4-foot,10-inch frame and get down to business.

She adjusted and readjusted the high-intensity goose-neck floor lamp that hovered over her lap, shedding a bright focused light onto her handwritten pages. Then, using her lighted magnifier, she read to Rick her newly authored work. Each day, he listened with care, asking questions to be sure he understood the events; then, with her diminished eyes almost touching the page, Mem reread the story slowly while he typed it into his laptop.

Both Mem and Rick were tea drinkers, traditions inherited from their respective mothers. Most afternoons, the aroma of sassafras or spiced tea wafted in the air; a round oak end table between them held their two teacups and treats to fuel them.

They worked and sipped together to squeeze her recollections between ink and page.

It was easy for me to eavesdrop from our large country kitchen that adjoined their nest. I loved the laughter and chatter coming from their exchanges. *There was magic happening in there!*

I was warmed by the privilege of these daily moments; of these irreplaceable times; of the intimacy of the space and spirit shared with these two remarkably brave souls—her carrying the cargo of her nine decades, and he continuing to forge his life through the known costs of stage four kidney cancer.

These were, indeed, times of grace.

In coming winters, this sweet scene became a ritual for all three of us. Mem's upstairs writing continued most mornings as did the afternoon transcription sessions, many melting right into the supper hour. Her growing album of writings became a passion for her and a mission for us.

Each year, when the snow finally ended, we opened the French doors as the spring breezes brought in the promise of warmer seasons. We moved from the glow of the fireplace to the openness of our long front porch where we felt the sunlight and enjoyed fresh fragrances. Eventually, Mem would return home to Tennessee for the summer and fall, but the story project did not abate while she was away.

This precious ritual continued, winter after winter, until she could no longer carry on.

My mother's advanced macular degeneration made reading, writing, and any close task difficult if not impossible, but her tenacity was exceeded only by her stubborn Scottish determination to keep on keeping on.

And keep on she did.

In her Phoenix-like spirit, through recoveries from a broken hip then two broken arms in her mid-nineties, till her death at ninety-eight, I witnessed the imprint of her dad as he lived a kind and generous life after crippling losses, honorably living the last decade of his ninety-one years despite illness and immobility. I saw in her shades of Lela, her orphaned mother from Texas, whose fierce creativity and resilience forged a family legacy. I saw in Mem a spirit that neither blindness nor age nor physical pain could douse.

Her spirit was unshakable.

So…our innocent attempt to keep my mother out of trouble while she was with us in Pittsburgh came to be a project of passion that rather innocently resulted in this book. Beyond her wildest intent, it will reside with us as a tribute to her courage and humor and grace.

But the blessing she was did not end there. This story project has been a gift of infinite worth to me. Through the hours and years of compiling and editing my mom's writing, I have come to really know her, and to know her in new ways.

Through her memories of her life, I know her now—not just as the woman who was my mother. I know her as my mother who was a friend, a fellow traveler, a role-model, an extraordinary individual and gifted teacher who was creative, courageous, nutty, unselfish, compassionate, authentic, generous, outspoken, and loving.

She was and remains a light and a treasure.

~~~ Mary Nelle McLennan,
2021

Rick and Memmie, December 21, 2001.

If I'm Not Alright, Don't Tell Me

"If I'm not alright, don't tell me." That was her sure-fire answer when asked how she was doing anytime during the last two decades of her life. Some folks still chuckle about that very Vivian-esque response, which she delivered without missing a beat.

"If I'm not alright, don't tell me," is appropriate, too, for the memories she collected and struggled to write, now saved and shared in this album. These vignettes are the memories, gathered over nine decades and penned into hardcopy by an alert woman in her nineties. They tell her story. They reveal her dreams, show her courage, and share how she experienced the times and people and places of her life. This is how she remembered it.

This album of memories is structured in five parts. The first introduces you to her family, the hardworking Bairds of Brighton, Tennessee. Part Two details the Baird Brothers Enterprises, a set of stores that served the Brighton community through nearly two-thirds of the twentieth century. In Part Three, you get to know many of Brighton's townspeople and their antics, kindnesses, friendships, and even their hate. She entertains you with true stories of foolishness and fun in Part Four. And in Part Five, we meet her as she grows into a gifted teacher, wife, mother, and mentor. To provide additional information or explanation, I have sprinkled "Dear Reader" notes throughout the stories.

Times and sensibilities are very different now than 100 years ago when my mother was young. Some of these accounts may seem inappropriate or politically incorrect by our current standards, but her actions and those of her family were never malignant or ill-willed or cruel. They were honest and of a different time.

Vivian's memories demonstrate that our southern accents show up in more than just the way we talk. Oddities such as eating "dinner" at midday and "supper" in the evening. Of knowing the difference between drummers and peddlers. Of living with the incongruities of a lady named "Clyde" and a young girl permanently nicknamed "Bill" because of a goat. Of a young boy called "Sugar Cat" or a pig named "Grunt" so the other pigs could say his name. Quirks like calling married ladies "Miss June" or "Miss Elizabeth" and referring to your minister as "Brother" despite no family relationship.

She also shows that our southern accents include foods with names that sound like construction materials and weigh almost as much—nuts and bolts; cheese logs and wrecking balls; dump cake. We consider pimiento cheese a staple and rely on sweet tea to wash it down. We long for tomato sandwiches in the winter, love chocolate gravy on biscuits for breakfast, and savor pot likker all year round. We nibble tea cakes and sip weak tea to make us feel better.

We understand where yonder is. We're always "fixin' to" do things, and we know well how to reckon. We enjoy our porches and take pride in our pooches. We dance like everybody is looking. And if we call you a bad name, we ask about your mama first.

We may not do things the way all y'all would, but those are our ways. And these were Vivian's times and memories.

So, as Vivian would say, if these stories don't match your memories—*don't tell me!* Just sit back and enjoy the trip!

~~~ MNMcL
2021

An Invitation to Readers

Stories surround us! They happen every day as they capture the history we create by living. Storytelling has been the heart of the human experience since early people began to utter language, but because stories are so natural, so "daily," we may fail to recognize their power. We share our personal experience and unstated knowledge through stories. They reveal the ways we intersect with people and events that happen as our lives play out. Our stories allow us to pass on what we've learned from life, what we value, and what we hope for.

Listening to the stories of others can spark our curiosity, and even simple ones may spur us to ask questions about our families, our communities, ourselves. In turn, the answers we learn may provide information or insight that shows us more about where we came from, where we've been, and where we want to go.

Not surprisingly, our stories often have missing pieces, blanks to be filled in. Unless we, as listeners and readers, puzzle about those blank spaces, unless we seek the absent how or who, the where or why, we miss out on a curiosity that can bring new information. Without asking questions, we risk losing treasures that may help us put things together in a new light and discover insights that could lead us to see the world and ourselves through a different lens. Often by asking simple questions about missing pieces we can learn scanty facts or juicy tidbits that help us fill in the blanks and uncover a wealth that might otherwise be lost.

We are fortunate to have detailed accounts such as the memories recorded in this book. But we need more, and we need to listen! The stories we hear and read may seem simple, and they may have missing pieces, but what they show is significant and worth saving. They give us a canvas on which we can paint the past.

Without stories to spur our curiosity—even sketchy stories with lots of blanks—there might be no one asking questions and searching for absent pieces about times and people and places that could too easily be forgotten. As a southerner might say, that would be a "crying shame."

So we invite you to seek stories! But we also invite you to ask questions! Be curious and stay on the lookout! Noodle around on history and genealogy sites; explore county records; snoop around for old letters, notes, receipts. Don't be timid about asking questions.

Without questions, even the blanks disappear.

~~~ *MNMcL*
2021

Vivian's Welcome

As I have looked back on my life of ninety-plus years, I realize that I have been twice blessed. I was blessed to be born into a loving and prosperous family where I had all that I needed for a happy and interesting life. I was also blessed with the ability to remember many of the fun and curious things that happened to my family and me.

I grew up listening to the many stories that both my mother and father shared with all of us. As a result, I felt that it was quite natural to tell stories, and I became a frequent storyteller myself. This was helpful in my role as a mother, an elementary school teacher for thirty-five years, and as a Sunday School teacher for even longer.

In recent years, my daughter, Mary Nelle, has encouraged me to put some of these stories in writing. With her help and that of her husband, Rick, I have pulled together some of these memories to share with you through this little book. I have not attempted to tell the story of my life in a chronological or comprehensive manner. Rather, I have tried to share with you a collection of special and fun memories that have stayed with me for all these years.

Through these stories, you meet my parents, Joseph Bryson Baird (known to many as JB) and Lela Gossett Baird; my brother Rudy; my sister LaNelle; and me as a child, teenager, and a young teacher, wife, and mother. You will also meet many of the residents of Brighton who were important to me as I was growing up. You will get a glimpse of what life was like in a small West Tennessee town in the 1920s and the years that followed.

I hope you enjoy these stories as much as I have enjoyed remembering them and sharing them with you.

~~~ *Vivian Baird McLennan*
2007

Mary Nelle and Vivian McLennan, Mother's Day, 2014.

Part One
The Baird Family — Who We Were

Lela Gossett Baird with her children,
Rudolph, LaNelle, and Vivian. c. 1920.

A Match Made in San Antonio

He left Brighton reluctantly, not knowing if he would live to return to his home in rural west Tennessee and the family he loved. Uprooted and stinging from the deaths of his first wife in 1901, then three years later, the loss of his second wife, Joseph Bryson Baird was in his early thirties and facing a frightening health crisis of his own.

Around the turn of the century, "JB,"as he was affectionately known, and his brother Knox operated a small general store in the community of Wrights, about ten miles from Brighton near the Dunlap area of Tipton County. JB's participation in this first joint enterprise was interrupted when he became ill with what was suspected to be Tuberculosis (TB), one of the most feared and deadly diseases in the world at that time.

In the 1800s and early 1900s, there was no reliable treatment or cure for TB, and it had become a tragically familiar disease to JB. It had taken his second wife, Effie Webb, only seven months after they married. This loss was an especially difficult blow for JB whose first wife, Minnie Sessum, had died from Typhoid Fever in 1901, leaving him with two young children—Ruby and Durell. In addition, his younger brother, John Robinson Baird, also suffered with TB, a disease which would eventually take his life on Christmas Day in 1912.

When JB himself became ill, Dr. Webb, Effie's father, recommended the precaution of moving to the dry climate of the southwest, which, at that time, was considered to help a person fend off the ravages of TB. Following this advice, JB found himself relocating to San Antonio, Texas.

As soon as he got settled there, JB visited Dr. John Hughes to pursue treatment for Tuberculosis. This began a lifelong friendship between the two men. It was also the start of a different approach to his illness. Dr. Hughes eventually determined that JB's problem was *not* Tuberculosis after all. Instead, surgery to JB's sinuses solved the problem, but his move to San Antonio turned out to have even greater significance…especially for my siblings and me!

While living in San Antonio, JB took a job as a conductor for the local streetcar company. Later he was promoted to the role of motorman—a rather heady job back then. He became well known for his good looks and welcoming manner and for entertaining his regular passengers on quiet nights in the city by allowing his streetcar to go full throttle down the largest hill on his route. This thrilled the passengers, and often a picnic atmosphere developed on his car.

As an observant motorman responsible for the safety and decorum of all his passengers, JB noticed an attractive young lady who became a frequent rider on his line. He learned that her name was Lela Edna Gossett and that she had grown up on a ranch near Devine, Texas. He also learned that she was attending finishing school in San Antonio while living with "Uncle" Gay and "Aunt" Lydia Buell who were friends of her father and late mother. Years later, Lela, who became my mother, admitted that she found many reasons to ride JB's streetcar because of its interesting and entertaining motorman!

When the time arrived for the annual motormen's picnic in San Antonio's Brackenridge Park, JB invited Lela to accompany him. A large photo that has been in our family for more than 100 years shows the well-dressed picnickers gathered for a group shot. The motormen actually wore suits and dapper straw "boater" hats. Their lovely dates wore long ruffled dresses and big fancy Victorian hats. Brackenridge Park became a favorite place for JB and Lela, and they spent many hours visiting—*and courting*—on the benches there.

JB Baird & Lela Gossett,
San Antonio, Texas, 1906.

In better health, JB returned to Tennessee in 1906 when Knox let him know about an opportunity to start a larger general store and related businesses in Brighton. In 1907, the two started Baird Brothers Enterprises, which grew over the next decades.

In January of 1907, Lela, who had just turned twenty-one, followed JB to west Tennessee, traveling three days to Memphis by train. I always heard that they married the very day she arrived, even before going to Brighton. I know for sure that, on January 23, 1907, they were married in Memphis by JB's friend, the Rev. W.B. Lindsay, a Presbyterian minister. For their wedding, Lela wore a white wool suit topped with a purple velvet shawl around her shoulders. As children, we were allowed to play dress up with her luxurious wedding shawl. The fringe on it felt like little tails that we loved to touch and tangle.

JB and Lela's first home was Brighton's Presbyterian parsonage, which they rented for a year or two. My brother Rudy was born in that parsonage in 1908. No one could have known then that Rudy would spend many years of his life involved in service to that congregation and to the town of Brighton.

Before my sister LaNelle was born two years later, JB and Lela moved to another house that they rented during the construction of their new home. Together they designed the new house following the architectural Queen Anne Cottage style popular in the first two decades of the 20th century.

JB had purchased most of the block between Murray Hill and the road to the west, which would eventually become U.S. Highway Route 51. He sold most of that land, but selected a prime lot for his own family's home on Brighton's main east-west street. Mr. Jimmy Hill built the new Baird home, a large white house with a deep wrap-around porch, just up the street from our stores. It was located beyond the north arch and west of Murray hill and remains the second house from the intersection of today's Woodlawn and the old Highway 51. Mr. Jimmy built several similar houses in Brighton, including one for Uncle Knox on what is now named Main Street.

Lela and JB moved their young family into their new house around Christmas 1910, but Lela would not unpack any boxes until they had decorated their Christmas tree! Daddy retold that story every Christmas, frequently kidding her about it and, starting long before each Christmas, asking her if it was time to decorate the tree yet.

My parents had three children together—Rudolph, LaNelle, and me, Vivian. All three of us spent our full and fruitful lives in the Brighton and Memphis areas. Our half-sister, Ruby, married, lived in Hughes, Arkansas, and had two sons who both became Arkansas legislators. She died at ninety-six in 1994. Our half-brother, Durell, married and made his home in Memphis. He served in WWII, but died of Tuberculosis as a young man.

Through five decades, JB and Lela were pillars of the Brighton Associate Reform Presbyterian (ARP) church and of the Brighton community. They reared their children in the heart of Brighton and lived the rest of their lives in the home they filled with activity, celebrations, music, love, and faith, all mixed with a great deal of foolishness and laughter. Fittingly, they both completed their earthly journeys right there, in the love of the family they loved so much—JB dying on March 27, 1962, at age ninety-one, and Lela, age eighty, on January 4, 1967.

Lela: A Lady Ahead
of Her Time

Texas takes great pride in its size. For many years before Alaska came into the Union, Texas was the largest of all the states. Texas cattlemen brag about their large spreads and the size of their steers. Even the nickname "longhorns" has the element of size built into it. Lela Gossett who came from Texas to Brighton to marry JB Baird, was small in stature—just over five feet, one inch tall—but her impact on her family, her church, and the town of Brighton was Texas large.

I know that my mother, Lela, was born on December 9 in Smiley, Texas, but there is uncertainty about the year. Some records, such as the US Census, show she was born in 1885 and several other records report 1886. Lela's father, Rufus Calvin Gossett, was born in Union County, South Carolina, in 1827 and migrated to Texas by way of Alabama and Arkansas. Judith "Judy" Roxander Carter, her mother, was born in North Carolina in 1847. Her family moved to Carrollton, Arkansas, when she was a child. At some point,

Judy relocated to Texas where she and Rufus married in1879, making their home in Smiley, Gonzales County.

In 1888, when Lela was about three and with two brothers under the age of eight, their mother died giving birth to twins, who also did not survive. Their father remarried and, in the 1890s, moved the family to a homestead and ranch near Devine, Texas, a new town that had just been started in 1891 on the South Texas plains.

In the first few years after the turn of the century, Lela was sent to San Antonio to further her schooling. She lived with"Aunt Lydia" and "Uncle Gay" Buell, who were family friends. I've always understood that it was during her time living with them that she developed her life-long ritual of having tea about 4:30 every afternoon.

It was during Lela's studies in San Antonio that she met and fell for Tennessee native JB Baird. He had moved to Texas as a remedy for a condition that the doctors believed to be Tuberculosis. After being declared healthy, he returned to Brighton in 1906.

Lela was twenty-one years old when she traveled three days by train from San Antonio to Memphis to marry JB. They wed in Memphis on January 23, 1907. JB and his brother Knox were working hard to build their retail enterprises in Brighton, and when Lela arrived, she jumped in with both feet to help the new establishments flourish.

All through her life, Lela shared engaging stories of growing up on her family's Texas ranch. She told of riding to school on her own burro; of armadillos, fields of beautiful Blue Bonnets, and spicy Mexican food; of their water supply pumped by windmills; and wild tales of the frontiersman Big Foot Wallace, an acquaintance of her father. She loved the lush green of West Tennessee, but never lost her love for the wide open spaces of her Texas home.

Lela threw herself 100% into anything she endeavored to do. She was talented, courageous, energetic. Always generous and thoughtful, she was a hard worker, a problem solver, and unfailingly open to trying new things. She was also a bit of a scamp, often playing pranks on all of us!

She was blessed with remarkable musical talent. In addition to her beautiful voice, Lela could play the piano and the organ, the guitar, the alto horn, a zither, and, on fun occasions, the Jew's harp. She had learned to play these instruments as a child with her musical family in Texas, and she brought her guitar with her when she came to Brighton.

Lela Gossett, circa 1905.

Although Lela grew up as a Methodist in Texas, she joined JB as a member of the Brighton Associate Reformed Presbyterian Church. She contributed her beautiful alto voice to the church choir and played both the piano and the church organ. Frequently, she and Mrs. Kerr, the minister's wife, would play a duet in church with Lela on the piano and Mrs. Kerr on the organ.

She also participated in a quartet of voices that performed in church on special occasions. In addition to Lela's alto tones, Mrs. Grace McLister sang soprano, Mr. Manuel Moose sang tenor, and the Rev. Robert Kerr sang bass. As a young child, I noticed that all of the members of the quartet wore dark-rimmed glasses, often call "eye spectacles" back then, so I started referring to them as the "Spec Quartet." The name began to catch on, yet I was surprised one Sunday morning when Rev. Kerr introduced them from the pulpit as the "Spec Quartet"!

Brighton had established an all-male brass band before Lela came to town. They provided entertainment for many community events and played occasional concerts. They also played every year at the town's big Fourth of July picnic in the bandstand on the school grounds. Lela and Mrs. Lula Jamieson were the first women to play in the all-male brass band. Not only were they the *first* two women to join the band, but for as long as I remember, they were the *only* two women in what was still called the all-male brass band!

In addition to being one of the first two women in that all-male brass band, Lela joined Mrs. Grace McLister in being the first women in Brighton to have their hair bobbed when they went to Memphis and returned with a new look that was becoming all the rage for women throughout the country.

Lela was also the first woman in Brighton to drive a car…

She was among the first women to vote in Brighton…

She owned the first electric sewing machine in town…

She was always ahead of her time.

For years, Lela taught a Sunday school class for the children of our church. She was a flexible teacher, sometimes taking the class with the youngest children and other times the teenagers' class. Sometimes she had the class meet on the lawn in front of our house. She also organized picnics for her classes and always presented interesting lessons.

Lela also had a green thumb and a magical touch when it came to gardening. She built flowerbeds all around the house and yard. From early spring to late fall, they were filled with bright blossoms. There were glads and hollyhocks; pansies, snapdragons, sunflowers, and many kinds of flowering shrubs. She often displayed bouquets of her zinnias and dahlias arranged in a conch shell that she used as a vase. Any time someone that Lela knew was ill, she would show up with a bouquet of homegrown flowers.

She also had window boxes on the house and hanging baskets on the porch, all dripping with colorful blooms. The concrete flower boxes alongside the front steps were always aglow with blossoms. She even took a World War I doughboy's helmet, turned it upside down, filled it with blooming plants, and used it for many years as a hanging basket in a tree just east of the kitchen windows.

When winter came, Lela could not be without her flowers so she dug a deep pit in the side yard and fitted it with doors that held glass windows. The resulting cold frame or mini-greenhouse was effective in keeping some of her flowers blooming all winter.

Like the rest of us, Lela was far from perfect. I remember one time when she was thinking about stopping by the farm that Daddy and Uncle Knox owned and used for growing corn that they sold at the store. She asked Uncle Knox if he thought the corn was ripe for picking, and he replied, "No it's not ready. I don't think you should pick it yet."

After Uncle Knox walked away, Daddy sidled up to her and quietly whispered that he thought the corn might be ready and that she should stop by the farm and check it out for herself. Though she did not want to go counter to Uncle Knox's advice, Lela really wanted some fresh corn, so she and I went home by way of the farm. She stopped, checked it out, then decided that the corn looked ready to her and that we could have some for dinner. After all, Knox would not have to know about it.

After picking an armful of corn and just before heading back to the car, Lela reached for one last ear that was up above her head. As she pulled down on it, the ear of corn slipped out of her hand and the stalk sprang back up. The corn plant swung around to hit her in the face, knocking her brand new glasses off and breaking them! Realizing that the next day she was going to have to face questions from Knox about what happened to her new glasses, Lela looked at me and wryly quoted from the Bible, "Your sins will find you out."

My sister LaNelle's daughter, Annette McCain Feaver, remembers another time when her grandmother Lela's frontier independence backfired on her. Lela had climbed high into a tree to pick some fruit when suddenly her footing slipped. Down she fell, head first—but she didn't hit the ground! Instead, she was wedged upside down in the fork of the tree! No one remembers how Lela was rescued, but we know that, fortunately, she was not seriously injured. When I asked Annette what else she remembers about that experience, my niece dryly replied, "She lived."

It shouldn't have ever been surprising to find Lela teasing and pulling pranks on family and friends. Playing jokes was one of her trademarks. One year as Halloween was approaching, she made a stand that held three cross-shaped figures and covered the crossbars with sheets to look like ghosts. Above the three ghosts, she arranged jack-o-lanterns with candles burning inside. As Halloween neared, the children in the neighborhood became accustomed to seeing the three ghosts in our yard. On Halloween night, Mother took the place of the ghost in the middle, so the children were quite shocked when one ghost came off the rack and ran toward them, arms flying in the wind! It was "Trick or Treat," and Mother provided both!

Lela always took a special interest in decorating for Christmas. Each year, she developed an original theme for the exterior decorations, and each year, her decorations were entirely new. As a part of her decor, she had Rudy build a large box that fit into the front bedroom window and extended several feet into the room. In this box, she sometimes displayed a nativity scene with figures about twelve inches tall that could be seen through the window. People came from far and wide each season to see what she had done. In her later years, Brighton sponsored a Christmas home-decorating contest. The first three years Lela entered, she won first place. After that, even though she continued to decorate, she did not enter the contest, wanting to give others a chance to win.

In 1966, Lela was gravely ill, but still, in her head, she was planning her Christmas decorations. That year, from her sickbed, she directed my sister Nelle and me to set up a simple vignette in the window box that Rudy had built. She told us to display a large family Bible open to the Christmas story in Luke. Beside the Bible, which was displayed on a deep blue cloth, she wanted a pair of antique reading glasses and an old Aladdin lamp that had been electrified. She specified that she wanted the lamp to burn throughout the holiday season. Like Lela, it was simple but elegant.

Lela Edna Gossett Baird died on January 4, 1967, in the Baird home with that lamp still glowing next to the family Bible in the window.

JB: A Good and Gentle Man

On February 12, 1871, my father—Joseph Bryson Baird, the son of Lucretia "Lou" McCalla and Robert "Bob" Stevenson Baird—was born in a farming area of northern Shelby County, Tennessee, near the town now named Rosemark. His growing up years were spent in the Almyra community of southern Tipton County along Beaver Creek Road. The family home place was located on the current site of the home of Russell McDaniel (a Baird/McCalla descendant) and his wife Dawn.

The Salem and Idaville communities were prominent in the Baird family's lives. JB and his siblings were educated at the Oak Grove School, which was run by Mr. S.O. Huey. I believe the school was near Idaville. Also, Bob and Lou and their children were faithful members of the Salem Associate Reformed Presbyterian Church where he served as an Elder. All but one of that family unit are buried in the cemetery there.

Sadly, I can't recount much about my dad's early years, although he used to tell us stories of those times. He spoke of getting up early to build a fire to warm the family on cold mornings, of riding back and forth to school on horseback, and about pleasant Sunday afternoon visits to his mother's McCalla family around Rosemark.

I know that JB, his father, and his five living siblings were grief-stricken when his mother, Lou, died in 1891 after giving birth to a child who also did not live. And he spoke of how they were again broken-hearted by the loss a few years later of his nineteen-year-old brother Leslie in 1897.

JB lived most of his adult life in and around Brighton. Following employment in several miscellaneous jobs, he and his brother Knox found their calling in the mercantile business. Around the turn of the century, the two brothers operated a small general store in the Wright's area of southern Tipton County, near Dunlap, and by 1910, they had established several thriving stores in Brighton.

Throughout his life, both love and loss came often to JB. He was twenty-six years old when, on January 6, 1897, he and Minnie Sessum were married. They lived on Byars Street in Covington, and he apparently worked at the Tipton Male High School. To their union were born a daughter, Ruby Lucille, on March 9, 1898, and a son, Joseph Durell, on May 29, 1901. Tragically, on December 11, 1901, at the age of twenty-seven, Minnie died of Typhoid Fever and was buried in the Salem Cemetery. JB not only lost his lovely young wife, but was left to handle the care of a two-year old daughter and an infant son. During the years immediately following Minnie's death, JB's stepmother, Hester Baird, and Mrs. Sessum, the children's maternal grandmother, helped care for young Ruby and Durell.

I'm certain that was a difficult time. All that was before I was born, and I don't know much about his life during those years immediately after Minnie's death. The Memphis City Directory of 1903 shows him as a streetcar conductor for the Memphis Street Railroad Company.

Joseph Bryson Baird, circa 1907.

JB found happiness again on January 27, 1904, when he and Effie Webb married. But, again, tragedy struck, and their happiness was short-lived when Effie grew very ill. Her father, who was a medical doctor in the area, broke the sad news to JB that Effie suffered advanced Tuberculosis. Her death came on July 15, 1904, only five months and eighteen days after their wedding.

JB himself had been suffering a lengthy illness that was thought to be Tuberculosis. Local doctors advised him to move to a healthier climate and suggested Texas. With his letters of recommendation and a train ticket to San Antonio, JB left Memphis shortly after his second wife's death. He sought treatment there, and eventually, the Texas doctor caring for him assured him that his illness, while serious, was not Tuberculosis.

JB stayed in San Antonio for a while longer working as a streetcar motorman where he met young Lela Gossett, a Texas native, and a match was made! Eventually, Lela took JB home to meet "Aunt Lydia" and "Uncle Gay" Buell, her guardians in the city. They gave their approval, considering him a "very nice young man."

In 1906, JB returned to Tennessee, his health restored and feeling well. Along with his brother Knox, they established two stores in the heart of Brighton—a general mercantile store and a separate hardware store. Named Baird Brothers General Mercantile and Baird Brothers Hardware, they were located across the street from each other, the general store facing north and the hardware facing south.

In mid-January 1907, twenty-one-year-old Lela Edna Gossett journeyed three days by train from San Antonio to Memphis. Upon her arrival on January 23rd, JB married his lovely young Texan.

In 1910, after renting for three years, my parents and their two young children, moved into a newly built home that the couple had designed together. The large white house was built and still stands east of the stores on what was called Baird Street (later officially named Woodlawn).

JB's retail enterprises grew over time. In addition to the stores he and his brother owned, he also established and ran a livery stable where he rented rigs and horses as well as selling horses and mules. The JB Baird Drug Company was "up the street," west of the hardware store. He also owned and ran an ice house beside the general store. He remained committed to these businesses and their customers until he retired due to age and ill health. The general store closed after decades of service to the community, and eventually my brother Rudy took over management of the hardware store.

Throughout his life, JB was active in the ARP church, first in Salem as a young man, then in the Brighton ARP Church for the rest of his ninety-one years. He was involved in numerous civic activities that supported Brighton and its surrounding communities. He always supplied and ran several food stands at the town's large Fourth of July picnics and the annual old soldiers reunion. In 1917, the year I was born, he and his brother Knox helped reorganize a chapter of the Knights of Pythias, a fraternal service organization founded in 1864 with the blessing of President Abraham Lincoln. Knox was the Chancellor Commander, and JB was the Outer Guard of the Brighton chapter.

JB enjoyed the company of others and loved a challenging card game. He always played a mean game of checkers, even in his final years. I can still see him and some of the men of Brighton playing Rook or checkers on a small table they would set up on the sidewalk in front of our general store.

Daddy loved dogs, and we always had at least one in the family. One of our family's enduring images of Daddy is him in a rocking chair holding one of his beloved dogs. In 1941, he had undergone a serious but routine surgery that did not go well, and he ended up spending about two months in a Memphis hospital. During that time, his faithful dog also became ill. The little pet was lethargic and nothing comforted him. Nothing, that is, until Daddy came home. As Daddy was being wheeled across the front porch on a stretcher, the pooch went wild! He jumped and barked and yapped and ran back and forth inside the house! Once the ambulance attendants placed Daddy in his bed, the little dog jumped up on the bed then burrowed under the covers beside him and stayed there for a long time.

Slowed by age, illness, grief, and loss of mobility, his final years were sedentary ones at home. Despite his disabilities, he was a serious but gentle figure for his four grandchildren: Annette, Lynn, Mary Nelle, and Buz. The three younger ones never knew him as the strong and active man he had been most of his life, and it was only years later that they realized he was kind enough to let them win at checkers!

Having lost his mother, his son, a beloved brother, and a young wife in the months of November and December, he was always solemn and pensive at Thanksgiving and Christmas. In spite of these deep losses and hardships, he lived his life as a generous and grateful soul.

My father, JB, was a tall, hard-working, honest man; a kind and big-hearted businessman who respected his customers and even carried some on credit when they could not pay, especially during the Great Depression. He was calm, level-headed, and always there for us. My siblings and I experienced his patience, kindness, and care as a loving father; we witnessed his loyalty and love for our mother; we were inspired by his steady commitment to our community.

Plainly said, my father, JB Baird, was a gentleman and a gentle man in every respect.

A Boot Box Baby

In January 1917, a huge snowstorm hit our small town of Brighton. While this part of western Tennessee usually got two or three snow storms a year, it was rare that more than eight inches fell at any one time. But then there are exceptions, such as the day I was born. About 2:00 A.M. on the morning of January 23, as more than a foot of snow was falling, Lela awoke JB and announced that it was time. Their third child was due, and Lela could tell that this would be the day, regardless of the snow or the storm.

At that time, our young cousin John Mann McCalla was sharing our home while he was working for my daddy at the Baird Brothers General Store. This cousin was a regular part of our family and helped out however and whenever he was needed. As Daddy got up and got dressed at Lela's warning, he alerted Mann who, of course, was sleeping, and sent him out into the cold to fetch the doctor.

Dr. William Alexander McLister's office was near the Baird's General Store, just past the arch east of our house. Not surprisingly, "Dr. Billy" was not in his office at 2:00 A.M., so

Mann had to trudge through the snow almost twice as far to get to Dr. Billy's home on the main street of Brighton.

Dr. Billy quickly bundled up and headed to our house. As a bonus, he brought along his son, Waldo Alexander McLister, who was also a physician. Along with Mann, Dr. Billy and Dr. Waldo made their way through the snow and up the hill to respond to Lela's call.

After Mann and the doctors got back to the house, Mann's next assignment was to gather my sister and brother, LaNelle and Rudy, and take them up the street to stay with "Grandma Phillips." Mrs. Phillips was not really our grandmother, but that's what we always called her even though, to this day, I don't know why. Lela had previously arranged for Grandma Phillips to look after my brother and sister when the time for my birth arrived, but no one had anticipated the snow. So, out into the winter storm Mann went again, this time with six-year-old LaNelle and eight-year-old Rudy in tow. My arrival was causing quite a stir!

As the morning progressed, I eventually arrived, although much smaller than anticipated. As Dr. Billy and Dr. Waldo sized up the situation, they were concerned that I might "get lost" and be too cold in the beautiful bassinet that Lela had decorated with lace and ribbons in preparation for the new baby. The doctors cautioned that they really needed a smaller, cozier crib to properly accommodate this tiny new baby. My dad had an idea, and now it was his turn to trudge through the snow. All wrapped up for warmth, he tramped to the Baird Brothers General Store and pulled from the shelf a large shoe box that contained a sizable pair of men's boots. He emptied the box, sized it up, and decided that it would be perfect as a snug place for the tiny new baby. Before leaving the store, he remembered to take along the extra ribbon and lace that Lela had requested.

Daddy trudged back up the hill through the foot of snow with his boot box and supplies. The doctors looked at it and agreed that it was just the right size to make baby Vivian safe and comfortable for the first few weeks of her life. Mother took the lace and ribbons and decorated the boot box to make it an acceptable substitute bassinet for my early days.

At the end of the day, Mann had one more task to accomplish so he returned to Grandma Phillips' house to retrieve my siblings, LaNelle and Rudy. He told them that there was a big surprise waiting for them at home and asked: "Can you guess what's waiting back at your house?"

LaNelle piped up with excitement, "A baby pig!"

I think—or at least I hope—she was remembering a litter of pigs that had recently been born in our barn. I hope she was not disappointed when she learned it was just a new little sister!

For many years, Mann would tease me about my being responsible for his having to go out in the snow on that cold morning in January 1917. Each time he told the story, the snow got deeper and the temperatures lower. As long as he lived, I called him each year on my birthday and had him tell me the story again. He always laughed about that day and loved to say that he knew me when I lived in a boot box!

Duck Well, Mama!

When I was growing up in the early 1920s, our family home, like many in our little town of Brighton, had a number of out-buildings. In addition to our house, we also had a barn, a coalhouse, a smokehouse, a henhouse, and the necessary outhouse. We no longer used the smokehouse for its original purpose. Instead, it had been remodeled and converted into a small house for our family friend and nanny Grace Fayne.

In our back yard, we had a "bored well." Unlike the larger wells that were dug out and lined with ceramic tile, a bored well was dug by a large auger until it struck water. The resulting well was much narrower than a typical well and required a very long, narrow bucket on the end of a rope to retrieve water. The well usually had a wooden top over it to keep anyone or anything from accidentally falling into it.

The well also had four large posts around the perimeter and a roof that sat on these four posts. This allowed us to draw water from the well and stay out of the rain at the same time. We referred to this little structure as our "well house," even though it had no sides or walls. A large wooden arm extended from one of the poles and held the rope when it was not being used. We were taught to *never* let the rope touch the ground and pick up dirt that would be transferred into the well.

Our hen house usually had about twenty hens in residence. Each spring, Mother would place a number of hand-picked eggs in the nests of these twenty hens. The hens would sit on the eggs for twenty-one days, and a new batch of baby chickens would appear. Then the henhouse would be filled with the cheerful "peep, peep, peep" of dozens of downy new chicks!

One year when I was still a small tyke, Mother decided to play a joke on one of the mother hens and on the rest of us as well. There was a Presbyterian minister who lived just west of Brighton and who did his preaching in some other town. As a hobby, Rev. White raised all sorts of fowl, including ducks. Mother obtained about a dozen duck eggs from Rev. White and placed them under one of the hens at nesting time. The three weeks of nesting proceeded as usual, but on the day of the hatchings, the sound of the "peep, peep, peep" was joined by a chorus of "quack, quack, quack"! We were all as surprised as the mother hen, and our mother had a good laugh on us!

One day, not long after the surprise arrival of our little flock of ducks, I came running into the house from the back yard. In my baby talk, I exclaimed to Mother, "Duck well, Mama! Duck well!" Mother realized that I was troubled about something so she raced into the backyard to see what had me so upset. After looking around the yard without finding anything alarming, she went out to the well and listened. She heard what I had heard—the distressed quacking of a duckling coming from deep in the well.

Mother sprang into action!

She ran back into the house and retrieved a small tin cup with a handle. She grabbed an ice pick and used it to poke holes in the bottom of the cup. On her way back to the well, she scooped up a handful of small stones and dropped them in the bottom of the cup to give it some weight. When she got back to the well, she removed the rope from the long, narrow bucket, which was hanging in its usual location next to the well. She tied the rope to the small tin cup with the holes in the bottom and lowered it into the well.

Mother gently moved the rope, fishing around deep into the well. In a short time, she felt a tug on the rope that was holding the tin cup, and which, she hoped, meant that the duckling had found its way into the cup. She gradually pulled the rope and the cup to the surface. As the cup rose from the water at the bottom of the well, the excess water drained out through the holes in the bottom of the cup, and the small duckling had a dry ride to the surface!

We kept this rescued duck and named him "Peeper," even though he was a "quacker." The story of my "duck-well" warning and Mother's ingenuity in saving the little duck was a *well-worn* story in our family.

How Vivian Became "Bill"

As a very little girl in the 1920s, I became friends with a billy goat that was a part of our family. He was more like a pet dog than a goat, and he frequently went with us when we were playing in various locations in the neighborhood. When we took him to fancy or public places, like Daddy's store, we would put a rope around the harness that mother had made for him so that we could keep him out of trouble.

One particular day with that goat is seared in my memory and "branded" me for the rest of my life.

During all my growing up, Grace Fayne, a black lady, lived in a small house on our property. She seemed like a part of our family and performed a number of jobs for us, helping Mother with the cooking and house cleaning, and, most importantly, she took care of us children on the long days while Mother and Daddy were operating the store. At her insistence, we children called her "Black Mammy," even though that term sounds harsh and inappropriate today. It was a term that we used with great affection, reflecting all that she meant to our family and to us children.

On hot summer days, Grace frequently took a gang of us on
long picnic adventures. She would not only take the three of
us young Bairds—Rudy, Nelle, and Vivian—but she would
also take the three DeWese girls as well as the two Johnson
children who lived a couple doors away. Our entourage was
completed by old "Bill Johnson" who was the Johnson
family's dog and, of course, we took our pet goat, "Bill."

Before we went on these picnics, all of the children would
make a special visit to Daddy's store to get our lunches. He
would give each of us a brown paper sack and allow us to
select what ever we wanted to eat on our picnic. With our
sacks filled with sausages, potted meats, bologna (otherwise
known as "baloney"), cookies, and cokes, we made our way
back up the hill to the Baird house where we met Grace.

Grace would lead this rag-tag group of eight children, one
large dog, and one billy goat up the street to Miss Fannie's
house, which was next to the present-day location of the
Brighton Baptist Church. Then we would trudge down the
lane toward our favorite picnic area, which was in the woods
behind Miss Fannie's house. To get to our spot, we also had
to cross a small stream by walking a long, large log that
spanned it.

The other children, all of whom were older than I, crossed
the log first. As the only preschooler in the group, I was
hanging back with Grace who would cross after I did. I guess
the drop from the log to the water below was really not all
that deep, but to my young eyes, it seemed large and
threatening. When it was my time to walk the log, I

approached the crossing with some fear and hesitation, but I had done it before, so I knew I could do it this time as well.

As I began to hesitantly inch my way across the log, Grace realized that "Bill Johnson," the dog, was already out on the log ahead of me. Before she could do anything about it, our goat, who'd been hanging back behind all of us, suddenly decided to remove the dog from the log! And there I was between the two of them!

As Bill-the-goat raced past Grace and charged across the log toward the Bill-the-dog, Vivian-the-little-girl was swiftly knocked off the log and down into the stream! I hit the water with a big splash, and all of the children, except for me, had a great laugh!

I was embarrassed and wet, but not hurt. Grace had brought a towel along, and she lovingly dried me off and assured me that all would be fine. I remember that my brown, lace-up shoes were all squishy inside. Even though I spent much of my childhood in overalls, this particular day I was wearing a dress. Grace removed my soaked dress, and I spent my picnic lunch wearing only my wet petticoat and panties, but I enjoyed it just the same.

The other children laughed all day about my being bumped into the stream. One of them suggested that since I had been caught in the contest between the two Bills—Bill-the-dog and Bill-the-goat—perhaps I, too, should be named, "Bill." So, from that day forward, my closest friends and most of my family have called me Bill. And, yes, even my

husband, who was also nicknamed Bill, called me that
throughout our fifty-three year marriage.

My older brother Rudy remembered and retold that story
for all of his life. He usually called me "Bill," but sometimes
he chuckled and referred to me as "Goat." Even as a ninety-
five-year-old living in an assisted living program near the end
of his life, he loved to tease me and tell his friends about how
his sister Vivian came to be known as Bill.

Baird children with the family's pet goat.

A Christmas Surprise

Dear Reader

In 2007, at the age of ninety, my mom shared this story as her Christmas greeting to her friends at home and around the country. This is the note she included with each letter she sent:

> *Christmas for me has always been a time of remembering. As this special time approaches, I am remembering you and all of my friends who have been so kind to me all year long.*
>
> *During my visit with Mary Nelle and Rick these past few months, I have had fun putting into writing some of the special memories of my 90 years in Brighton. It gives me pleasure to share with you one of these stories about a Christmas experience that has stayed with me since my childhood. I hope you enjoy it.*
>
> *I wish you a very Merry Christmas and a New Year filled with good health and happiness.*

Here is the story she wrote:

As my dad, JB Baird, learned in 1910, decorating for
Christmas was a top priority for my mother, Lela. They had
just moved into their newly built home in Brighton, and
decorating for Christmas was the first thing she did, even
before unpacking the moving boxes!

The holidays were always busy times at our stores and
required long working hours, yet our family always made
time to put up a beautiful Christmas tree—always, *except* for
the year when I was seven years old. That's what made that
year so unusual and so special.

It was late December of 1924. Christmas was fast
approaching, yet we had no tree in our home. The
Christmas party at the church had already taken place.
There were lots of decorations at our family's store and
other decorations all around our house, but a Christmas tree
had not appeared. We three children—Rudy, Nelle, and I—
continued to remind mother that we had no tree. Each time
we did, she explained that she and Daddy had been very
busy at the store and that bad weather had prevented us
from making our usual family trip out to the farm to chop
down a tree.

As Christmas day neared, our worries increased. We asked
mother what would we do if we did not get a tree before
Christmas. Where would Santa place our gifts? Mother
reminded us that Dr. Hurt's family, who lived next door,
never had a tree, yet they always had a nice Christmas. We
could not argue with the point she made, but we were
worried nonetheless.

Christmas Eve arrived, and Daddy was still busy at the store. People continued to come in for their gift shopping, and he kept the store open until nine o'clock. Mother was home making the usual boiled custard and jam cake, two requirements for our Christmas celebration, especially as treats for Santa Claus. Many of our traditions were in place, but without a Christmas tree it seemed empty!

Finally, bedtime neared, and we began to worry even more. This just didn't seem right! We asked mother, "Is Santa going to stop here if we don't have a tree? What if he doesn't stop?"

Mother assured us, "Just hang your stockings on the mantle. We will put out the boiled custard and jam cake for Santa. I'm sure he will find us and everything will be all right."

The three of us kids were still worried, but we trusted her and got ready for bed. The night passed quickly. Along with the visions of sugarplums, worries about Santa danced in our heads. "What was he going to think about our not having a tree? Would he be disappointed in us? Would he leave us any presents?"

As was our custom, we children awoke before the sun came up. Mother came to our bedrooms and invited us to come to the front room where in years past Santa left our presents. I remember how cold the floor felt to my bare feet as we made our way from our bedrooms to the front of the house. And I still remember my concern about what we were going to find —or what would *not* be there.

As mother ushered us into the front room, our jaws dropped! We stood there in disbelief and awe! There, in front of us, was the most beautiful Christmas tree I ever saw! *Ever*! It was covered with shiny, store-bought ornaments and tinsel. Mixed in among the fancy ornaments were our homemade ones that we had made in years past. Many of these were those prickly little balls that had fallen from sweet gum trees and which we had wrapped in silver foil we'd saved from sticks of Juicy Fruit gum. Red and green roping looped around the tree. And most amazingly, many limbs held silver scalloped cups holding real burning candles. The glow of the candles gave the room a warm and inviting yellow aura that pulled us in and assured us that a wonderful Christmas had arrived!

Santa had found us after all! Mother feigned surprise, saying, "Look what Santa brought!" Our presents were mounded near the tree! We were thrilled!

As happened most years, Santa brought new robes, night gowns, and house shoes. Mother always made the gowns and robes even though Santa Claus got the credit. We quickly put on the new robes and house shoes as protection against the December cold. One year, Nelle and I got "twin" robes made of soft, pink flannel outing with little blue flowers. The fabric looked familiar to me, and I mentioned to Mother that I remembered seeing the cloth in Daddy's store. She assured me that Santa always shopped at Baird Brothers stores. That was good enough for me!

That year, Santa brought me a "big" tricycle. "Buddy," as I called my older brother Rudy, helped me mount this larger trike and taught me to scoot to one side so my young legs would reach the pedals. After that, I did fine on my new vehicle until I got to those raised strips of wood that covered the small cracks where the floors of rooms joined. I couldn't maneuver my tricycle to go over them. I still remember Buddy showing me how to stand up and lift the front wheel over the bump! After learning that, I spent Christmas Day riding from room to room, all through the house—around and around and around!

Santa had left a wonderful selection of other toys under our tree, but also a nice collection of fireworks. As was our tradition, Santa brought us firecrackers, sparklers, and Roman candles. Before the sun came up on Christmas morning, we took our Roman candles out onto the front porch and launched them into the neighborhood, shivering and shaking while enjoying this exciting tradition.

Looking back, I remember the beauty of the burning candles on the tree, but I'm also reminded of the danger they posed. Of course, we did not have electric lights back then, and the lighted candles brightened the dark room before the sun came up. I remember a later year when the lace curtains on the window near the tree picked up the flame of one of the candles and started to burn. Mother immediately saw the fire and raced to pull the burning curtain down from its rod. She rolled the lacy fabric into a ball even as it burned and used its length to smother its own fire. Mother was always in charge, always alert, and we always felt safer when she was around.

Our mother and father—and Santa, of course—gave us a very merry Christmas that year and for years and years to come.

Whoa! Whoa! Whoa!

Our family belonged to Brighton's Associate Reformed Presbyterian Church, and going to Sunday School was an important part of every week for us. We would always dress to look our very best, and this included making my patent leather shoes as shiny as possible. To shine my shoes, I would go to the pie safe and retrieve a cold biscuit and then go out on the porch and sit on the floor with my legs hanging over onto the first step. I'd cut the biscuit in half and rub the inside of the biscuit all over my shoes. The oil in the biscuit would make the patent leather shine nice and bright. It worked like a charm!

Sunday School began at 10 A.M., and we tried never to be tardy. The first church bell would ring at 9 A.M. Daddy never failed to follow the ringing of the first bell with an announcement, "The bell says it's time to get ready for Sunday School." The bell would toll again at 10 A.M. If we were still at home, Daddy would announce to all, "The bell is saying we are late!" That meant a scramble!

Mother sang in the choir each Sunday. While she was in the choir loft, which was behind the minister and facing the congregation, she made me sit in a pew where she could keep an eye on me. One time during a regular service in the winter, my friend Helen DeWese and I were sitting in the sanctuary and enjoying playing with the nap on Helen's new coat. We took turns running our fingers along the nap and smiling about the new designs we were creating on the coat each time. We were paying more attention to that game than we paid to the service, and mother noticed. She subtly shook her head "no" and that quieted us for a short time. Then we started playing with the coat again. A second time, she signaled us to stop playing. Again, we did…for a short time. When she saw us playing our new game a third time, she quietly got up from her place in the choir loft, and, in a very dignified manner, descended from the choir, walked across the front of the church, and down the west side aisle to our pew. She signaled us to move apart from each other and sat between us where she remained for the rest of the service.

When the service ended, and we walked out of the church toward our car, I expected to feel the full wrath of Mother's displeasure. She said nothing. We drove home and I was sure she would let me have it then. Again, she said nothing. All day long, I thought I was going to hear about my bad behavior, but nothing was said. Mother knew that the suspense and anticipation of how I was going to be punished was worse than any punishment she could give out. Years later, she confirmed that this was her strategy—and it worked.

In the 1920s, the congregation of our Brighton ARP church outgrew the building where I first attended. In 1923, they built a new church nearby. Once the new building was

completed and in use, the former church was sold to a
Baptist congregation and moved on wheels to a new location
in Shiloh, just a mile or two south of Brighton. Sadly, the
new ARP building burned in 1938 and was a total loss. Our
Uncle Knox was the Chairman of the church's Deacons and
served as Chairman of the Building Committee for a new
worship site, which is the pretty brick church still in use
today.

Following the completion of the new church in 1923 and the
removal of the old structure, all that was left of the old
building was an outline of the foundation made up of short
concrete blocks that once supported the church. Daddy and
most church members parked their cars in a vacant lot that
was east of the new church, just behind where the old
church had been.

One evening following a night service, my family walked
through the dark to our Model T Ford, which was parked
behind the church. As usual, we three children piled into the
back seat, and Mother took her regular seat next to the
driver. Daddy went to the front of the car and cranked the
motor to get it started. Then he hurried to the driver's side
of the car where there was not a door but a stationary panel
over which the driver had to step in order to enter the
vehicle. Once Daddy got into his seat, he pressed down the
clutch, pulled down on the gas lever, and away we went.
Almost immediately, we heard a terrible thump and felt the
car bump roughly into two or three solid objects! Then we
all heard that awful sound of metal crunching against
concrete! Daddy was as surprised as the rest of us, and he
immediately pulled back on the steering wheel and hollered,

"Whoa! Whoa! Whoa!" as if he were still driving a team of horses!

Other people coming out of the church heard the awful noise and came running to see what had happened. It was a very dark night so some of the other men turned their cars around and fixed their headlights on our car. That's when we discovered the cause of the terrible thuds—there we were, driving through the concrete block remains of the old church! Daddy was shocked! He could not imagine how he had miscalculated his path back to the driveway and ended up among the concrete blocks of the old foundation.

Mr. Manuel Moose and Mr. T. D. McLister along with other men of the church helped Daddy pull some of the blocks out of the path of the car and also helped pull the bent fenders away from the tires. Soon we were out on the driveway and headed home, although a little worse for the wear.

As we headed down Main Street, Mother, who had sat quietly fuming at this embarrassing incident, finally spoke up. *"Whoa? …Whoa?… Whoa?"* she asked boldly. *"JB do I have to remind you that you are driving a car—not a horse and buggy?"*

It was a lesson learned and just one of the adjustments folks had to make as, like the whole world, Brighton changed from horses to cars in the 1920s.

A Dark, Dark Night

It had been a very busy day at the Baird Brothers stores. Christmas was fast approaching, and people were buying toys and other gifts at the Hardware Store. The General Store across the street was also doing a brisk business. Every day, Dr. Frist, a friend of my dad, wrote a weather column in the Memphis Commercial Appeal, and he had predicted that our area was going to be hit by a major storm with extremely cold weather and very strong winds. As still happens today, the prediction of bad weather brought people to the store in large numbers. Everyone wanted to be well-stocked to ride out the storm. The staff at the store—Mother, Daddy, Miss Clyde Huffman, and Ralph McDaniel —were exhausted.

As the weather became more threatening, the skies darkened. Even though people were still coming in to stock up on groceries, Daddy suggested that Mother and Miss Clyde begin to head for home before the storm got worse. Mother found me asleep on a pile of overalls, as often happened. She shook me and told me to wake up because we were heading home early.

We went out to the car that was parked in front of the store, facing west. Mother tried to start it, but it would not budge. She tried repeatedly, but had no luck. Daddy came out and tried, too. Nothing worked. Daddy went back in for a tea kettle of boiling water. Sometimes when the engine was frozen, he would pour hot water on it, and it would start. He raised the hood and poured the water onto the engine. But not this time!

Nothing that Daddy tried helped start the car, so Mother decided it was time for her to walk us children home if we were to get inside before the worst of the storm. She grabbed one of the kerosene lamps that hung along the side walls of the store in those days before we had electricity, and she, Rudy, LaNelle, and I began our hike through the arch and up Murray Hill toward home.

The wind was howling fiercely, and Mother feared that it would blow out the flame in the lantern, leaving us to journey on in the dark. To keep the lantern glowing, she held a piece of cardboard near the top of the chimney on the side from which the wind was coming. As we walked along, Mother kept our spirits up by saying, "This is the darkest of nights, but we will conquer the darkness."

I remember walking along the wooden sidewalks, holding Mother's arm and my head bowed down against the wind. The planks in the rough, uneven sidewalk were about ten feet long, and they ran east and west parallel to the street. In this hunched posture, I noticed for the first time the gaps between the boards that made up the sidewalk. All of these boards had been sawed at Chisolm-Dewese Sawmill that we passed on our left as we climbed up Murray hill.

As we neared home on this trek through the cold wind, mother announced, "Home at last; home at last." To this day, I remember how good that made me feel. As soon as we got inside the dark house, she lit the lamps and carefully adjusted the mantle in each one to brighten each room. Soon the Aladdin lamps worked their magic, and the house was glowing. The lamps' warm light and our mother's courage were a welcome refuge on that dark, dark night— and an inspiration for the rest of my life.

Lela Gossett Baird, circa 1950s.

The Green Nash

In 1929, Daddy bought a brand new Nash automobile. I was convinced then, as I am now, that he bought it as a reaction to Mother's outrage at the Nu Enamel fiasco—but that's another story. I'll tell that one later.

The new Nash was a beautiful dark green color with a subtle black stripe outlining the windows. This was one of the first cars in Brighton that was not black in color, except, of course, for our Nu Enamel car.

The Nash was a two-door model. The front passenger seat was engineered in such a way that the back folded down so the entire seat could be flipped toward the driver to allow passengers access to the back seat.

This was our first car with glass windows that rolled down and up. It also had shades that could be pulled down above each side window to block the sun. I remember, too, that it was our first auto with a windshield wiper that could be operated by the driver or the front-seat passenger. This single wiper was positioned at the top of the outer face of the windshield. Inside the car, the top of the windshield had a black knob for manually moving the wiper back and forth. I remember Mother leaning over to operate the windshield wiper when Daddy drove us in the rain.

Inside the Nash, there were two vases for flowers, one on each side of the car, mounted just rear of the door. The beautiful amber carnival glass vases gave the car a special touch, and Mother took great advantage of that. We never traveled without flowers in those vases! For much of the year, Mother would clip flowers from her own garden before each trip. Sometimes, she would do this at the last minute as we were getting ready to go and everyone was piling in the car. During the winter, she would use straw flowers that had been grown and dried by Aunt Martha Ann, an African-American lady in our neighborhood.

Riding in the green Nash always made me feel special. I especially remember one Sunday when we were on our way back from a visit to my half-brother, Durrell Baird, who lived in Memphis. Mother, Daddy, and I were ensconced in the back seat with the dome light on, while my brother Rudy drove and his friend Gerald Hindman rode up front. We took that occasion to ride up and down the streets in several of Memphis' nicest neighborhoods, including a trip past the sprawling "Pink Palace" with its opulent Georgian marble exterior. That enormous mansion, now a museum, was originally the home of Clarence Saunders, founder of the Piggly-Wiggly chain, our country's first true self-service grocery stores.

We loved that car so much that when Daddy was ready for his next new car, the green Nash was driven to the barn behind the house and stored there. My dad made no effort to find a buyer, and it remained unsold for many years until someone finally came forward with a nice offer to buy it.

How I wish we had it now!

Stormy Weather

For many years, the DeWeese family lived next door to us, just west of our home on the street now called Woodlawn. The DeWeese family consisted of Walter and Ola and their three daughters, Helen, Alene, and Kathryn. Our two families did many things together, but one routine really stands out in my mind. Miss Ola had grown up with a terrible fear of storms, and she passed that fear along to her girls. Whenever it stormed, Miss Ola and her three daughters would come over to our house. I don't remember how it started, but we could depend on the fact that, when a storm blew into Brighton, the DeWeese family, except for Mr. Walter, would show up at the Baird house…even in the middle of the night.

These "storm parties"resulted in a lot of fun—and memories. Lela, my mother, knew how to put Miss Ola and her daughters at ease, and we children enjoyed the process. The first thing that Mother did was to put a feather bed down on the linoleum floor of the hall. This provided room enough for all us kids to sleep on the floor together. Then Mother would hang a sheet over the doorway that led from the hall into one of the bedrooms. Next, she would place a lighted kerosene lamp on the floor behind the sheet, which was a sure sign that some silliness was about to begin.

The light of the kerosene lamp shining behind the suspended sheet provided a screen on which Mother projected her menagerie of "shadow animals." With her nimble hands and fingers held in a variety of positions, she was able to call up many different animals. I remember a donkey with a mouth that moved for eating and talking. There was also a rabbit that moved rapidly across the screen and a bird that flapped its wings.

Mother taught Miss Ola how to make animals, too. Together, the two of them produced stories featuring a variety of animals that appeared on the screen, each with a voice and personality all its own. Before we knew it, the storm had ended, and we all fell into a peaceful sleep.

Thanks to my mother, we had talking "movies" long before the other kids in our town!

Camping Our Way Back to Brighton

Road trip! Road trip! In 1926, my brother, sister, and I traveled with our parents in our new Ford Model T Touring Car from Brighton, Tennessee, thirty miles north of Memphis, to San Antonio, Texas, to visit my mother's family. The three-day journey covered a distance of more than 800 miles—quite a jaunt, even on today's interstate highways. Back then we had only local, mostly unpaved roads that zig-zagged through the countryside, and most of them weren't marked or even named.

We arrived safely at the home of my mother's brother "Azzie" (Francis Asbury Gossett) and his wife Zora in San Antonio. All five of us visited Mother's family for our first week there, then Daddy returned home by train so he could tend to our family stores and business. The rest of us continued our month-long visit with our maternal relatives. We visited lots of aunts, uncles, and cousins and also the small town of Devine where my mother grew up.

Three weeks after Daddy had gone back to Brighton, it was finally time for us to go back home as well. With help from our Texas kin, Mother, Rudy, Nelle, and I packed up the

Model T for our return drive to Tennessee. We made quite a sight—our pretty, adventurous mother; three kids ages nine, fifteen, and seventeen; a newly acquired German Shepherd puppy; and a sack of fresh Texas onions secured neatly on the running board! Somebody even made a "Home or Bust" sign for us to display on the car!

The Baird caravan is on our way from San Antonio to Brighton, Tennessee, in the Model T. (1926)

The four of us retraced that same rough and unmarked route during the day, remarking on the changes in the countryside and picnicking from our packed supplies. But nights along the route were a challenge, especially for a woman traveling alone with her children.

As each day wore on and dusk neared, mother's attention turned to finding a place for us to stay. There were not many inns or motels along the highways nor were there parks or camping facilities where we could stop over. We chugged along in that Model T, but as daylight began to wane, mother would scout for a home that "looked friendly." After spying a home where she felt we would be safe and the residents might be open to the idea of strangers sleeping in their yard, she approached the front door of the chosen home.

Erect and proud, she would knock on the front door. She would announce, "I am Lela Baird from Brighton, Tennessee, and I am traveling back home with my three children. May we have permission to camp for the night in your front yard?"

She always offered to pay for the privilege of camping. Amazingly, her request for a camp site was never refused! And her offers to pay for the privilege were never accepted. Our only responsibility was to leave the place as we had found it, which, of course, we did.

After receiving permission to overnight in the homeowner's yard, the four of us would pitch our tent and unroll our sleeping mattresses, then settle down for the night. Our "chamber pot" was available to take care of our "necessary functions." Each morning, mother would always find a discrete place to empty it.

Throughout the nights in the tent, Mother kept "Texas," the new puppy, close to her so that she could muzzle his growls or barks when he started to alert us to sounds that he thought suspicious. We kids slept well.

In the morning, mother would fix breakfast on our camp stove, just as she had for our suppers. When we were packed up and ready to leave, she would thank our hosts, then we would continue camping our way back to Brighton.

It was all quite an adventure for a nine-year old girl! But looking back as an adult, I marvel at the courage and audacity of our independent mother to make that 800-mile trek under the daunting travel conditions of the 1920s.

I'm standing on the ferry that carried us across the
Arkansas River during our Texas trip. I had been
awakened from a morning nap at my request so that
I would not miss the excitement of the ferry ride.
Apparently, I had not taken the time to
adjust my knickers!

Dear Reader—An Invitation to Ask Questions,

My mom wrote about their return trip from San Antonio when Lela traveled with the three children and a puppy named "Texas." JB, who had traveled with them on the way west, had taken the train back to Brighton a few weeks earlier so he could tend the stores. I find it interesting that Mem didn't tell us about the trip to Texas when the family of five traveled together, and I find myself wondering how the trip was different when my Granddaddy JB was along. Who drove? How many hours a day did they jog along in their Model T? Where did they stay overnight? Did they camp along the way? Where did they buy gas? How did they know which roads to take? So many questions and no one left who knows the answers!

Questions like these are vital, despite the absence of those who could provide the answers. Listening to others' stories, especially the memories of our elders, and asking even simple questions allows us to uncover the beauties, the aches, the truths of daily lives that will someday be gone. Collecting, recording, writing the answers are ways to save people and places and times from being forgotten.

~~~ MNMcL

Lady in the Hall

When I was eleven years old, my brother Rudy was finishing his second year at Bryson College, a Presbyterian school in Fayetteville, Tennessee. The college was located about 250 miles east of Brighton, in the lovely rolling hills south of Nashville. It is a beautiful area, and the campus was filled with impressive red brick buildings. Quite a few Presbyterian youth from the Brighton, Atoka, and Salem communities attended Bryson, including my sister LaNelle who went there as a Freshman in 1929.

Because of the distance to Fayetteville, we did not get to see Rudy very often during the school year. I was excited when in May of 1928, after I was out of school for the summer, Mother and Daddy announced that we would be taking a ride to Fayetteville to bring Rudy home for the summer.

We also had another reason for the trip. From their days as young boys, Daddy and H.H. Robison—or "John"as my dad called him—had been friends. John had pursued a career in education and, in the second decade of the 1900s, he served as the Superintendent of Tipton County Schools. Starting in 1919, he taught as a professor and President of Bryson College. Dr. and Mrs. Robison invited Mother, Daddy, and me to visit with them and spend a couple of days on the campus before Rudy was ready to go home.

I remember being so impressed that we would be staying with Dr. Robison, the President of the college. Before I got too enchanted with that fact, my dad decided to have a little fun with me. He told me that, while it was certainly impressive to meet the President of the college, that the college had actually been named after himself, Joseph *Bryson* Baird. For a while I almost believed him, but then, by the twinkle in his eye, I realized that he was just teasing me—again!

For our first night there, we stayed on campus with the Robisons. Although I was impressed with meeting the President, I made the observation to Mother that his suit needed ironing. She explained that he was wearing a special lightweight suit—probably seersucker—that was made for the warm weather, and that it was supposed to look that way.

The next day, I had the courage to tell President Robinson that I was disappointed in my visit so far. Surprised, he asked, "Why is that, Vivian?"

I was honest and replied, "I had really wanted to stay with Rudy, my special buddy."

It's always good to have friends in high places. By the end of the day, Dr. Robison had arranged for me to stay in Rudy's room in the dormitory!

Of course, in those days, the dormitories were segregated by gender, so when I first walked into the dormitory, I heard a startling announcement over the loud speaker. "A lady is in the hall!" I quickly looked around and saw only my brother, so concluded that I was the lady they were referring to! Imagine that! They called me a "lady"! For the rest of my visit, each time I wanted to leave Rudy's room, he was required to step out into the hall and, in the loudest voice he could muster, announce, "Lady in the hall!" This was all part of the fun for me!

Rudy's roommate Calvin Smith was nice enough to move to a room next door while I was there, and he allowed me to use his bed in the same room with Rudy. If my brother was not in class, I was with him. He very kindly allowed me to go everywhere he went.

One afternoon, Rudy borrowed Daddy's 1926 Model T Ford to go into town to pick up something he needed. He asked Calvin, Hick McDill, and one other friend to go with us. As we were driving along, he began to tell his friends about my driving experience two years earlier when we were visiting in Texas and I decided to show my cousins that I could drive. His friends were stunned and really didn't believe that I could drive.

"She can't drive this car. She is too short to even reach the pedals!" they retorted.

They thought that Rudy was just making it up, but he knew how to make them believers. He pulled over onto a side street where there was less traffic, got out of the driver's seat, and said to me, "Scoot over." I moved under the steering wheel, and he got back in and sat beside me. I stretched to put my feet on the pedals, put my hand on the gas lever, pulled it down, and away we went down the street!

The friends were amazed, and now they were believers. At the end of the block, we stopped so Rudy and I could change places again, and we continued on in to town.

The next day, Mother and Daddy and Rudy packed the T Model with all of Rudy's belongings, and we made our way back to Brighton. Returning home, I now had a new nickname—"The Lady in the Hall."

And it was the only time I'd ever stayed in a men's dorm…so far!

One summer day several years later, Rudy's college friend Hick McDill, whose real name was Albert, came riding into Brighton and pulled up to our house on a motorcycle. He spent the night with us and remembered me as "The Lady in the Hall."

While Hick was there, I let him know that I had never been on a motorcycle, so he offered me a ride. In spite of the fact that he had been impressed with my driving skills, he was not about to let me try to drive his motorcycle! However, he did take me for a ride. We roared through Brighton, Hick in the front and me holding on for dear life behind him!

That ride with Hick was the only motorcycle ride in my life…so far! And we've yet to see about a second night in a men's dorm…

Dig Under or Crawl Over

One of the characteristics of my younger years was that I was accident prone or maybe foolhardy—*or both*. On more than one occasion, these traits led to visits to Brighton's "Dr. Billy" McLister, and each one alarmed my parents. Early on there were numerous small injuries and a broken arm, but two big ones that happened while I was in high school stand out from the others.

A collision between a car and a log truck at the corner of our street and the newly built Highway 51 had left a large pile of logs near the intersection. The pile was just laying there waiting to be picked up by its owner. As Nell Hindman and I made one of our frequent after school trips to Phillips Grocery Store and Restaurant, we came upon this large pile of logs. Nell had the good sense to go around them. I, however, preferred the route over the top. As I was carelessly climbing over the logs, the piled shifted, some of the logs rolled, and one pinned my ankle. Not only was I hurt, but I was trapped! Seeing my problem, neighbors stopped everything and ran to rescue me.

After being set free by the neighbors, I ended up at Dr. Billy's office. He was unable to fix the injury to my ankle and referred me to Dr. Dickson, an orthopedic specialist in Covington. Dr. Dickson put my broken ankle in a cast, which hobbled me for quite some time. Sadly, this resulted in my having to sit out Brighton High's whole basketball season. I was a short-but-fast guard on the school team, and I really hated to miss playing because I loved the game and enjoyed wearing my red and white basketball uniform.

Not long after that fiasco, I found myself in Dr. Billy's office once again due to another spill caused by my own silly exuberance. On a cold winter day, I was really excited when my boyfriend, Winfield McLennan, better known as Bill, turned up at our house driving his Dad's brand new car. In my excitement, I did not take the time to walk down the steps from our front porch to the driveway like a normal person. Instead, I jumped over the last several steps, forgetting for the moment that there was ice on the sidewalk below. I landed on my wrist and knew immediately that I'd hurt it badly. As my friend Elizabeth Kendall would later say, I guess Bill could tell that I was really falling for him. *(groan)*

Once again, Dr. Billy referred me to Covington's Dr. Dickson, the same orthopedic specialist who had cared for my fractured ankle. Before we left for Covington, I remember my dad expressing his exasperation with my many accidents and injuries. He told Dr. Billy that he was going to have to build a fence around me to keep me safe.

Dr. Billy dryly responded, "Well, it won't do any good, JB. ... This one would either dig under or crawl over."

Grandmother's Spool Bed

I never personally knew any of my grandparents. Despite that, they were not completely absent from our lives; stories and memories my family shared brought them to life for me. This story tells the travels of my paternal grandparents' parlor bed, which knew both life and death, and how it came to be mine.

In November of 1891, my father's birthmother—Elizabeth Lucretia McCalla Baird—gave birth to a child who did not live. Two days later, she died at the age of forty-three from complications of that childbirth. Several years later, my grandfather—Robert S. Baird—married Hester Stevenson, a widow; together, they raised the younger Baird children who had been left without their mother.

I do not remember Grandfather Baird because he died in 1919 when I was two years old, but family stories about him lasted long after he was gone. Our family often chuckled about how he and his second wife Hester parted ways, literally, when it came to church-going. The Baird and McCalla families had for generations been staunch Associate Reformed Presbyterians (ARP). Grandfather Robert was a "dyed in the wool" ARP, having served as a Deacon and an Elder at the Salem ARP church. In 1903, he became a

charter member of the Covington ARP church and served
as Ruling Elder there. Hester, however, belonged to the
Covington Presbyterian Church. Fortunately for the couple,
these two churches were about a block apart, so that allowed
them to ride together in the buggy to church on Sunday
mornings, then park midway between the two churches and
go their separate ways to worship. After the services, they
would meet back at the buggy and make their way home for
Sunday dinner. We always thought that was funny!

I still hold some very special memories associated with my
visits to our step-grandmother Hester Baird in Covington.
Our family would often spend Sunday afternoons visiting
Grandmother Baird at her home and of course at the
holidays. When I was about nine years old, I started going
for solo visits with her and my cousins who lived with her. To
get there, I would hitch a ride with Mr. Fleming on the
Standard Oil truck when he headed back to the depot in
Covington after refilling the kerosene reservoir at Daddy's
general store. What made this such an adventure was that
there were no doors on the truck!

I remember climbing up into the passenger seat and Mr.
Fleming connecting a leather strap that stretched across the
opening to keep me from falling out. I would hang on for
dear life as we rumbled along the road to Covington. He
would stop that big truck at the end of the street on which
Grandmother Baird lived, and he would help me down off
the truck. Then he would sit there and watch as I walked up
the street to Grandmother's house, carrying my little suitcase
with what I needed for an overnight stay. As I got to within
sight of the house, I would hear Mr. Fleming's truck start up
when he knew I was safe.

When I stayed over night with Grandmother Baird, I would sleep in a bedroom on the second floor to the left of the stairs as one ascended from the main floor. Across from the top of the stairs was a second-floor parlor, and just down the hall was the bedroom where Grandmother Baird slept. For some reason, I was fascinated with the high bed in which she slept. It was a very old spool bed, and the mattress was four feet off the floor. It was so high that I had to use a step stool to get up onto it! My daddy remembered that this bed originally had a trundle bed underneath it, but the trundle was gone by the time I became aware of the bed.

According to family accounts, this spool bed made the trip with the McCalla family from their early days in South Carolina to Georgia, then to middle Tennessee and eventually to the area of Shelby County now known as Rosemark. Lucretia's parents, Robert and Nancy McCalla, gave it to Lucretia and Robert when they married on August 22, 1867.

It had been a parlor bed before it was given to Lucretia. Parlor beds held a very special significance at that time. Back then, sleeping rooms and social areas were often linked or even the same room. It was typical for a family to have a bed in its parlor where guests were received and where they spent much of their time. Such parlor beds were used when a family member was sick and needed to be cared for. They were also used for childbirth and the recuperation period afterward. Before hospitals were convenient, the parlor bed was frequently the place where family members spent their last days on earth.

The Baird's spool bed really captivated me. I loved it and even told my daddy, "If I'm still living when Grandmother Baird dies, I would love to have that bed."

Daddy replied, "If I'm still living when Grandmother Baird dies, I'll see that you get it."

A few years later, in 1939, when I was twenty-two and teaching in my first job at Burlison Elementary School, Grandmother Baird passed away. True to his word, Daddy arranged for me to inherit Grandmother's big bed.

After I got it home and because of my lifelong interest in working with wood, I decided that I would strip off the brown enamel paint and then stain the bed's natural wood. After working diligently on it out in the back yard, I discovered, much to my chagrin, an awful coat of blue paint under the ugly brown coat. I tried to strip off that coat as well, but found it too hard a job for me to tackle. I finally broke down and had it taken to a woodworking shop in Covington where I paid $15 to have it stripped by a professional. After the work was finished, the man who did it said that it was the hardest paint-stripping job he had ever done.

Once all the paint was removed and it was stained a rich walnut color, I took the bed home and set it up in my bedroom in my parents Brighton home. I could hardly wait to sleep in it for the first time. The first evening that we had the bed in my room, my mother, father, and brother Rudy fell into discussing how many of my ancestors, including both my Baird grandmothers, had died in that bed. I knew they were teasing me and trying to get me going, so I just brushed it off. Finally it was time to go to bed. How I had looked forward to my first time to sleep in the long-coveted spool bed!

As I lay in the bed thinking about its long and significant history, I began to hear low, soft moaning. I wondered what that noise could be. First, I thought it was coming from outside. As it continued, though, I came to realize that it was inside instead. Then I realized the moaning was coming from under the bed!

I crawled down out of bed and turned on the fancy new light that Mother had bought for me and clipped on the headboard. The moaning continued.

Cautiously, I bent down and peeked underneath the bed. Whoa! I was shocked! There, to my great surprise, was my mother Lela, the ultimate jokester and the source of all the moaning!

It really should have been no surprise to find Mother under there because playing pranks was her trademark. And she had gotten me again!

Grandmother's spool bed has remained one of my treasures and a connection to my ancestors even though I didn't know them. When Bill McLennan and I married in 1941, this became our bed in our home in Clopton. It has stayed in our home the rest of my life, and someday it will belong to Mary Nelle.

Part Two
Baird Brothers Enterprises

Men admiring a car in front of the JB Baird Drug Co.
and the Baird Brothers Hardware, circa 1910.

Baird Brothers General Mercantile

The Baird Brothers Enterprises, a partnership between my dad, JB Baird, and his brother Knox, were a large part of our lives and of the life of Brighton, Tennessee, in the first half of the 1900s. The Enterprises consisted of the General Store, the Hardware Store, the Ice House, the Livery Stable, and the JB Baird Drug Company. My parents spent most of their time in the General Store, and I frequently tagged along. It was "home base" for my childhood.

The General Store building, which faced north on what is now known as Woodlawn, was about thirty feet wide with tall double doors in the middle of the front and large glass windows mounted on a wood base on either side. A tall person could look in the windows from the sidewalk, but to enter the store, you had to go up three concrete steps to a small porch that was just slightly wider than the double doors and about three feet deep.

When you entered the store, you were in a wide center aisle. Actually, it was the only aisle for customers' use. It ran all the way to the back of the building and led to the back door where goods arrived in delivery wagons and, eventually, in trucks. A traditional potbelly stove sat in the center of this wide aisle. It was a "Warm Morning" stove, a popular brand at the time. On cold mornings, Daddy would dump two scuttles of coal into the stove, and then it really lived up to its name. It would get so hot that the stovepipe would glow bright red. Lela, my mother, would see red, too, and holler at Daddy that he was going to burn down the store. He never did, and we enjoyed the warm mornings.

The walls on both sides of the store were lined with wide, built-in shelves that reached all the way to the ceiling. These were always stacked with goods—groceries on the right side of the store and shoes, clothing, dry goods on the left. Waist-high in front of the shelves, there was a long working counter that allowed the staff to temporarily stack goods when they were filling the shelves or retrieving items for customers. Large glass showcases that were accessed from the rear were located in front of some of the shelves. Only "select" customers were allowed behind the counters to choose their own items from the shelves.

On these open counters, Daddy always kept a large roll of pink wrapping paper that had the words "Baird Brothers" stamped about every twelve inches. I especially remember Daddy placing large bolts of cloth on the counter and cutting a segment for customers. Once the material had been cut, he folded it into a small square and wrapped it neatly in the readily identifiable pink paper. My siblings, Nelle and Rudy, frequently talked about receiving packages from home when they were students at Bryson College in Fayetteville, Tennessee. Even before the names on the packages were called, they could recognize a pink package in the pile and know there was something for them.

A Kid in a Candy Store

Sweets were always part of the General Store's inventory. In the position of honor, on the right side just inside the front door, was the kids' favorite display—the candy showcase. It was my favorite, too! People entering the store were always tempted to stop there first.

Having a family who owned a general store had many advantages. For one, I tended to have access to something that all my friends and classmates wanted—candy! I was always allowed to help myself to candy from the showcase, and I would frequently show up at school with a sack that I would share with my friends, especially a schoolmate named Ruby who shared a double desk with me. Since we sat so close together, it was hard for me to slip into my bag of treats without offering some to her. Ruby would play upon my sympathies and tell me how she wished her family had enough money to buy candy. This led me to help myself to even more candy from the showcase so that I could bring enough to help satisfy Ruby's impoverished sweet tooth along with my own. Before too long, Daddy noticed that his supply of candy was dwindling faster than his profits were rising. After a little sleuthing, he discovered that I had begun to supply many of my classmates with free candy! He then made it clear that I was welcome to take any candy I wanted for myself, but that he was not in a position to supply the whole school!

There were many kinds of candy to choose from and hard choices to make. The colorful showcase included wrapped candy bars—Milky Way, Baby Ruth, and Zero. Loose, by-the-piece coconut candy came in many colors—pink, green, yellow, and more. A rainbow of temptation! And it cost only a penny a piece! Of course there was chocolate—plenty of chocolate—in squares and in kisses. There were also wax shapes filled with different colors of syrup. These came in the shapes of animals, cars, people, and just about everything else. I especially remember the little wax pop bottles filled with different colors and flavors of syrup. One gulp and the syrup was gone! The wax left behind was good for chewing, but mother insisted that it was bad for our teeth.

On top of the candy case, there was a special, smaller glass case for gum, and I took a particular interest in this one. As a little girl, part of my job at the store was to keep the case straight and pretty. The sticks were not all the same size, and I took pride in arranging them in stair steps according to the various lengths. Juicy Fruit was the longest. It was my favorite, wrapped in silver foil with shiny red letters. I remember when a new brand named Dentyne was introduced. The "cookie man," who supplied some of the sweets we sold, also supplied gum. One day he brought Dentyne signs that he stuck on the walls all around the store, inside and out. I became so attached to that small gum case—one might say I was "stuck to it"—that it still sits in my living room today. All the gum has long since been chewed, but my memories remain sweet.

It was exciting when the traveling salesmen called drummers would arrive with their suitcases and show off their new products. I remember the day the "cookie man" unfolded his case and displayed many kinds of yummy-looking cookies. My eyes grew big, and he could tell that I was interested. He invited me to help myself. As I moved to take him up on the offer and reached for a cookie, I discovered that all of these sample cookies were *glued* to his sample case! Everyone had a good laugh on me! The kind drummer did have a few "real" cookies with him and rewarded me for being the butt of his joke. I thought it was worth it!

Ladies' and Gent's Departments

On the left (east) side as one entered the store, there were glass cases featuring a limited array of ladies' clothing. While the store didn't carry dresses, skirts, and blouses, it did offer a nice selection of various "unmentionables"—underwear, lingerie, and stockings, both silk and cotton. The next showcase on that same side held jewelry arranged in large trays. There were brooches, rings, hatpins, bracelets, combs, and more. We had many different vanity sets consisting of brushes, combs, mirrors, containers for lotions, and jars with pretty tops. We called them "toilet sets" back then. I remember, as a girl, opening the jewelry cases from the back and trying on all sorts of beautiful pieces. I was in heaven!

One time a representative arrived to demonstrate the process of engraving names and initials on rings that were especially designed for the engraving. These rings had a flat surface across the top that spanned the width of the finger. Here he would engrave whatever the customer wanted. He set up his equipment in the front part of the store where everyone could see him work, and he sold a lot of engraved rings that day.

A curious collection of embroidered scenes on cloth, framed and suitable for hanging, were also displayed in these same showcases. I fell in love with these fabric pictures and felt I just had to have one. I remember pestering Daddy for one of these framed embroideries until he finally gave in. The one I chose was a scene of swans floating on the water in front of some pretty trees. It still hangs in my bedroom today.

Shelves above the showcases along the left wall of the store displayed a diverse selection of bolts of colorful cloth suitable for making dresses, curtains, or just about anything a lady wanted to sew. There was also a wide collection of ladies' shoes and slippers. Moving beyond the aisle that was used for getting behind the cases, there was another counter along the center aisle of the store. The wall behind this counter held a collection of men's shoes and boots. This counter held a large selection of blue Bulls Eye brand overalls, There were all sizes for men and many sizes for children. Not only was I fascinated by these products, but it was also my favorite place to nap! I have long remembered the drowsy feeling when my mother would shake me awake as I lay on a comforting stack of overalls. Calling me by my nickname, she would say, "Wake up, 'Bill.' It's time to go home." I dreaded going out on those cold evenings after I'd been sleeping so warm and comfortably on a bed of overalls!

A Baking Powder Challenge

A large "Calumet" clock hung on the east wall of the store, at the end of the aisle between the ladies' and men's shoes. This large wind-up clock would run for seven days with just one good winding. The word "Calumet" was written in large gold lettering on the glass covering the clock's face. This clock, which for years hung in my office at home, always reminds me of a "baking soda demonstration" at the store. A representative who was selling a new brand of baking powder, Clabber Girl, came to demonstrate the superiority of his product over the old standard, Calumet. He set up a long table on the patio that ran in front of the store just off the sidewalk. On this table, he placed two glasses of water and a bottle of vinegar. After putting vinegar in each of the two glasses of water, he then put a spoonful of Calumet baking powder in one and Clabber Girl in the other and demonstrated that Clabber Girl would make the glass of vinegar bubble up more than Calumet did. He then invited those observing the demonstration to try it themselves. Each time they tried it, the customers seemed to agree that the Clabber Girl produced more bubbles. After that, my daddy sold both brands!

Kerosene and Molasses—Pour Your Own!

At the back of the store, along the south wall, there was a large square metal container that held kerosene for sale. This reservoir was about four feet tall, and it had two spigots and a crank. People would bring their own cans or containers when they came to buy kerosene. Most would bring five-gallon cans for their purchases. To get the kerosene, they would place the cans on the floor underneath one of the spigots that was designed especially for large cans. Other people would bring smaller cans, usually one gallon. They would place these smaller containers on the top of the kerosene reservoir and stretch a hose up to that level to fill them. To get the kerosene to flow from the reservoir into the containers, the customer, or sometimes Mother or Daddy, would crank the pump to start the kerosene streaming.

The kerosene reservoir was near the back door of the store so that it could be easily filled by Mr. Fleming, the driver of the Standard Oil supply truck. He would drive in behind the store and drag a supply hose from his truck into the back door to refill the reservoir. After replenishing our supply, he would head back to the depot in Covington. When I was about nine years old, the refilling of the kerosene offered me still another adventure. My Grandmother Baird lived in Covington, and I enjoyed visiting her and my cousins who lived with her. Rather than disturb my parents, I would hitch a ride with Mr. Fleming as he returned the big tanker truck to the depot.

At certain times of the year, our store also offered a pour-your-own dispenser of delicious Rock Island Sugar House molasses. It was a rare and prized treat, but I'll leave the details of that for another story.

Social Circle around the Potbelly Stove

The general store was a gathering spot for many of the people of Brighton. On cold days, the older neighbors would sit around the glowing potbelly stove and tell stories. Neil

Bell was a favorite with the stories of his experiences during World War I. There was one particular episode that people really enjoyed and would ask him to retell. He told in lively fashion of jumping into a ditch one dark night and huddling up with another soldier who was also scared and looking for shelter. After he built up all the details and suspense of his story, Neil delivered the punch line…when daylight arrived, he discovered that the other guy was a German soldier! And they were both shocked!

Some afternoons after school, my brother Rudy and his friends would gather at the store and loaf there until it was time to go home and milk the cows. These guys had a tendency to sit on one of the two counters where people would place their goods while they completed their shopping. Rudy was always asking his friends to get off the counter so the customers could use it, but it was a constant battle until he happened upon a very clever-but-devilish solution. First, he drilled very tiny holes in this counter top at the approximate locations where the guys usually sat. Then he somehow rigged up a device using pins and string. When he pulled the hidden string, these very tiny, very sharp pins would pop up through these holes right where the guys were sitting! His friends couldn't figure what was causing the uncomfortable pinches in their bottoms from time to time, but eventually they stopped sitting on the counter!

A Wager on a Wedding

A second advantage of hanging around the general store came from the fun I had wagering with my dad. One day I overheard him in conversation about Miss Janie DeWese, whom some regarded as an old maid at the ripe old age of twenty-four. She had been dating Mr. Tom Murray for some time, and, in spite of everyone's expectations, they had not become engaged.

One day, I overheard Daddy say to someone in the store that Janie and Tom would probably never get married. I piped up and said that I would bet him a pair of new overalls that they would. Daddy said that he would take that bet, but then he wondered out loud, "What makes you so sure?"

I had to confess that I had "inside information." Janie was the aunt of my friend Helen DeWese and lived with their family. When I was spending an overnight with Helen, we overheard a conversation between Janie and Tom who were sitting in the parlor. Helen and I were playing in the adjoining room and, unbeknownst to them, we were privy to their conversation! Before Helen and I adjourned for the night to our quarters on the sleeping porch, we heard them making plans for a wedding.

Even after I confessed to my dad about what we'd overheard, I'm not sure he thought there would actually be a wedding. But, when the couple got married a few months later, I got my new pair of overalls!

A Surprise from Memphis

Whenever Daddy would travel to Memphis to buy goods for the store, his custom was to bring back something to each of us three children. On one particular day when he was going to Memphis, I was not well, and Mother had decided that I was too sick to attend school. Before leaving, Daddy came to my bed and asked me what I wanted him to bring home to make me feel better. I remembered that a few days earlier when I was staying overnight with my friends Eunice and Louise Billings, Mrs. Billings had served us Grape Nuts for breakfast. That was a real treat, and I really loved them, so when Daddy asked what I wanted him to bring me, I said that I would really like some Grape Nuts. At least that's what I *thought* I said.

When Daddy returned at the end of the day, he came to my bedside and proudly presented me with a beautiful round, yellow GRAPEFRUIT. I was shocked! "But that's not what I wanted," I mumbled. "That's what you asked for," he told me. The next morning, Mother cut the grapefruit for me and I, of course, had to eat some just to be polite. I had never liked grapefruit, and that morning, I was vividly reminded why. It was so sour that I had a wince on my face for the whole day! Surely, Daddy had made a mistake; I was sure I had said "Grape Nuts."

Quick Thinking, JB!

Occasionally, I was expected to contribute to the running of the store by handling small chores that were assigned to me. Every once in a while, Daddy would ask me to clean up the piles of stuff that had been tossed on to his desk. I would sort the various papers and put certain kinds of letters in their appropriate stacks and put other papers in some of the pigeon holes and small drawers on the top portion of the desk.

One day, when I was approximately ten years old, I was cleaning off the desk and found a box of strange looking "balloons" in the top drawer. For some time, I had been aware that Daddy would frequently go back to this corner of his desk with some of the gentlemen who would stop into the store, but I was never certain about the apparently confidential business that they were conducting. When I found the box of balloons, I took one to Daddy and asked him what it was. Daddy didn't miss a beat as he explained that occasionally he would cut his finger while trimming a piece of meat. This, he said, would require that he put a bandage on his finger, and, of course, it was important that this bandage not get wet. He explained that these long thin balloons would cover his finger and keep his bandage dry.

As a ten-year-old, I bought it! I found this explanation perfectly satisfactory and put the balloon back in the box with the others. A few years passed before I found out that these balloons were really condoms and were *not* used to keep bandages dry at all!

Animal Rescue

Hanging around the store infused me with an entrepreneurial spirit at an early age. One day a gray cat showed up at the store. When no one came to claim him, I put a sign up on the makeshift chalk board in front of the store, "Gray cat for sale." Shortly after that, Mr. Wooten from Munford stopped by the store looking for his missing dog. He saw my sign advertising a gray cat for sale and asked if I would put on the board a sign announcing that his dog was missing. I agreed and within a few days, Mr. Wooten's dog showed up at the store. Daddy called Mr. Wooten to tell him the good news, and soon he returned from Munford to claim his dog. To show his gratitude, Mr. Wooten gave me $2.50 to thank me for putting this sign on the board. I was in business!

Dear Reader,

This is where "Mem's" handwritten story stopped. It didn't really have an ending summary or closing thought like she usually included, so I believe she meant to add more stories from her remarkable memory. Thanks to her tenacity in putting her memories and these stories on paper despite her severe vision loss, we, who now shop at mega-merchants, big box stores, and online, have a vivid picture of the shopping experiences our families had 100 years ago when she was a child. And, as her daughter, I now treasure the Calumet clock, the framed embroidery scene of swans on a lake, and, of course, the small glass showcase that held those sticks of gum.

~~~MNMcL

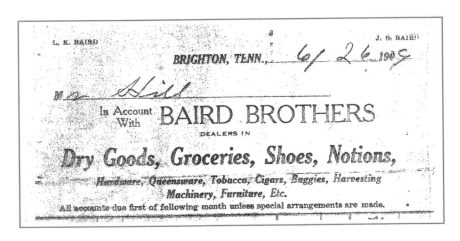

Hardware, Home Goods, and Horses

Across the street from our General Store and facing south, stood a two-story building that was painted white. A large sign that no one could miss extended even higher than the second floor. It boldly announced "Baird Brothers Hardware" in huge black letters.

Uncle Knox, my dad's younger brother, looked after the Hardware Store just as Daddy (JB) looked after the General Store, but both brothers owned equal title to both businesses. While Daddy looked the part of a general store keeper—no suit coat, shirt sleeves rolled up—Uncle Knox always came to the hardware store in a dress shirt, coat, and a tie anchored by a beautiful diamond tie tack. He was never without that tie tack, and usually added a flower in his lapel. Uncle Knox rarely got his hands dirty, but hired people to do the work of the hardware. He preferred to hobnob with customers and the bigwigs of the county.

The front of the hardware store had a double door in the center with a large window on each side. When you entered, there was an office area on the right. It was set off from the rest of the store by a wall, probably to protect the safe that was inside the office and to keep customers out. Customers entering the store could look into the office through an opening in the office wall and greet Uncle Knox who was usually busy at his adding machine. Within the office and mounted on the wall to the right of the opening was an array of "pigeon holes" used by the staff to sort and store papers that related to orders and inventory.

Baird Brothers Hardware sold everything from building materials, animal feed, coal, tires, farm implements, dishes and cookware, lamps, gasoline, oil, kerosene, and, at Christmas, toys and giftware. Merchandise was displayed in three sections of the store. The center section was directly in front of customers entering the double doors. This section was separated from two others by long aisles that ran from the front of the store all the way to the back.

On the east wall of the store, which was on the right when you entered, there was a large inventory of actual hardware. Open kegs held nails and screws of all kinds and sizes, nuts, bolts, tacks, and the like. There were plumbing supplies, latches, switches, door knobs, drawer pulls, lock sets, fencing wire, and so on. There was also a selection of "smoothing irons" for ironing cloth. These were the heavy, triangle-shaped kind that had to be heated on a wood or coal stove.

Past these goods, there was an open counter where people would deposit their purchases while they completed their shopping. On the north end of the counter, there was a cash register as well as small scales for weighing bags of nails and other small pieces that were sold by the pound.

Baird's Hardware had its own potbelly stove that sat just beyond that east counter, about halfway to the back of the store. The coal-burning stove was surrounded by a collection of mismatched chairs. Cushions were thrown on top of unopened kegs of nails to allow people to prop themselves and engage their neighbors in the latest gossip or political discussions. In the winter, neighbors and customers hovered around that stove as much for the lively talk as for the warmth.

Just beyond the stove, another set of double doors, even larger than the ones at the front, opened the east wall to the outdoors. Through these doors, supplies were delivered and customers loaded large orders of grain, animal feed, or fencing wire directly onto their wagons and trucks. This wide opening helped cool the store in the hot summer months.

A big selection of field tools—rakes, hoes, shovels, pitchforks, cotton scales, and the like—hung on the east wall at the back of the building, just north of the large doors. I remember the first time the salesman from Orgill Brothers Wholesale amazed us all by showing us a new product, a yard broom. This was a large fan-shaped tool that made the job of gathering leaves much easier than previously when we used garden rakes for that purpose.

The center counters were stocked with seasonal goods and gear that greeted customers when they walked in. At Christmas, a colorful display of holiday decorations for the home as well as giftware and items to please homemakers filled that central area.

The left or west wall of the store offered housekeeping goods of every kind. The tall built-in shelves held a large assortment of pots, pans, dishes, flatware, and all sorts of other housewares. Two shelves further along the wall going north were filled with oil lamps. Many of the lamps had beautiful glass shades with pretty colors and some with scenes on them. I especially remember one with roses that were raised on the glass, and I loved to feel the shapes of the roses.

At the far back corner along that west wall, there were two large stacks of mattresses. I was able to climb on one stack and then use it as a boost to get to the higher stack. Up there, I had a bird's eye view of the store and a comfortable place to curl up and sleep when I got tired!

As Christmas time approached each year, I remember bright-colored displays of toys along that west wall. Naturally, I was especially interested in these products! I asked Uncle Knox why people needed these since Santa brought toys on Christmas. He assured me that these toys *belonged* to Santa who would see to it that they got to the children.

Large burlap bags of feed and grain were stored along the back wall of the Hardware—chicken feed, cow feed, and others. They came in rough burlap bags that we called "tow sacks." These feeds gave the hardware a sweet smell of grain. People could buy an entire bag of feed or scoop out smaller amounts, as they frequently did with chicken feed. A larger scale for weighing the feed sat on the floor at the back of the store near the big double doors.

Also along the back wall were the stairs that went up to the second floor. The area up there was used mainly for storage and was not open to customers. Frequently, I was allowed to use that upstairs area for riding one of the tricycles that was stored there for future sale. As you can imagine, this created an awful noise for the folks downstairs! Once a customer asked Uncle Knox how he was able to tolerate this racket overhead. His answer was that it was better than having to dodge me on the tricycle all the time. *I was quite offended!*

There was a long trough of water outside the Hardware Store and to the east. Customers who arrived by horse and wagon would take their horses to the trough to drink while they shopped. I remember one family who drove their wagon all the way from Salem to Brighton, a distance of more than five miles, to shop at the Baird Brothers stores. While Daddy appreciated the business, he sometimes grumbled about the "presents" this family's horse left outside the store while waiting for his owners. Mother reminded Daddy that he needed to be grateful that this family came all that way to patronize his stores—and he was.

Baird Brothers Barn

Daddy also ran a livery stable, which consisted of a barn and a modest supply of horses and buggies for hire. He also sold horses and mules. The barn was located on the street that ran alongside the railroad track and southwest of the General Store.

Traveling salesmen and other visitors would ride the train to Brighton and stay at the Majestic Hotel there in town, but they needed transportation to travel to the businesses where they sold their wares. They would rent a horse and rig from Daddy for their travels around the countryside beyond Brighton.

I remember Mr. Jess Moore, a kind drummer who visited our area frequently. Like many traveling salesmen called drummers or peddlers, Jess would arrive by train. He would call ahead and reserve his favorite horse, which he called "the little bay mare." Daddy would oblige and have the horse and rig waiting at the depot when he arrived. Jess would take a room at the Majestic Hotel and use the rented horse and buggy to travel to the country stores east of Brighton. The next day, he would use the same horse and buggy to visit the stores west of town.

JB Baird, circa 1910.

The goods that the local stores ordered from these drummers would be shipped from Memphis to Brighton on the Illinois Central Railroad. Shopkeepers would send an employee to the railroad with a wagon to pick up the goods when they arrived.

Looking back, I'd say that my dad, JB, was the Hertz or Avis of his day!

Dear Reader,

For centuries and even through the middle part of the 1900s, drummers and peddlers were a common and colorful part of life, especially in rural areas where stores were remote and it required a long transit to go shopping. Both peddlers and drummers were traveling salesmen with a major difference in what they sold and to whom. Drummers were itinerant representatives of wholesale companies who sold goods to merchants and store owners for retail sale to their customers. They showed their wares in catalogs and in sample books. Many drummers sold to the Baird Brothers stores, and some became real friends of the family.

On the other hand, peddlers were individual sellers who traveled from house to house offering small household goods and tools that they carried with them. In early Europe and in early America, they usually carried everything in packs on their backs as they walked from settlement to settlement. More enterprising peddlers traveled and lived in wagons that also served as a warehouse—like the "professor" depicted in The Wizard of Oz. *Peddlers were welcome visitors to many isolated homes as were the goods they offered—and the gossip they brought! Their wares were simple items necessary for daily life such as scissors, pins, needles, buttons, ribbons, thread, razors, brushes and combs, soaps, small tools, cooking utensils and spices and flavorings. These traveling salesmen had a dramatic impact in developing the consumer economy we have today.*

~~~ MNMcL

The Ice House: Playing It Cool

The Ice House, also owned by the Baird Brothers, sat just east of the Baird General Store. It was a small building with no windows and just one door. For years, horse-drawn wagons delivered big blocks of ice from the ice plant owned by Mal Smith in Covington.

The ice came in 300-pound blocks. The size of these huge blocks slowed the melting process as did the practice of spreading sawdust over the ice. My dad obtained the sawdust from the DeWeese-Chisolm sawmill right there in town. The ice house held a big rake and a large scoop as well as several pairs of huge tongs and an ice saw. The scoop was used to throw large amounts of sawdust over the ice, and the rake was used to spread it evenly.

Using an ice saw, the 300-pound blocks were cut into blocks of twenty-five or fifty pounds for customers to purchase. The ice saw and the big tongs from the Baird Brothers Ice House are still in our family.

As I was growing up, many a game of chase involving children of the Baird, DeWese, Hill, and Robertson families ended in the cool ice house. There, hot and tired children would cool off by sitting on huge blocks of ice that were damp and cool and covered in sweetly fragrant sawdust. It was a wonderful refuge from the humid summer heat.

Eventually, our neighbor, Will Hindman, bought a truck and started delivering ice in Brighton. After Mr. Hindman got his truck, he and his son Leroy drove around and sold ice from the back of it. As young Leroy would drive from house to house, he would sing out, "Ice man! Nice ice man! How much ice do you need today?" When customers were ready to buy, Leroy would rinse the sawdust off the ice using a water supply that he carried on the truck and then deliver it to the customer.

In my mind, I often hear Leroy's sing-song call for ice as I think about his death as a soldier during World War II.

Burglars at Baird Brothers General Store

I guess that, at eleven years old, I just assumed that it was natural to have a big, loud burglar alarm in your family's living room. Our family did, and it was a large metal hemisphere mounted behind the door of the "parlor" in our home on the street now called Woodlawn. When something triggered it, a strong hammer repeatedly struck the big bell with a sound that was—well—alarming. It was for the Baird Brothers General Store; having such an alarm did not seem strange to me because it had been there as long as I could remember. At 1:00 A.M. one warm spring morning in May 1928, while my family and I were fast asleep, the burglar alarm sounded. Something was wrong at the store! My nineteen-year-old brother Rudy was the first out of bed to turn off the alarm. My dad hurriedly dressed and cranked our wooden wall phone to summon the Sheriff, Mr. Jim T. Scott, who lived seven miles away in Covington.

Our store was located on the same street that we lived on, and it was less than a quarter-mile east of our house, which was on a hill. Even though the store was close, the view was blocked by two features—one natural and one man-made.

The main line of the Illinois Central Railroad passed between our home and the store, and when the track was constructed, a levee was built through Brighton to elevate the track across the falling landscape of the town. Fill dirt that had been excavated when the railroad was built through the hills of Atoka, five miles to the south, was hauled in to create the Brighton levee. All the townspeople called this "the dump," and many still do.

The builders carved several tall arches or short tunnels in this massive structure so the east-west streets of Brighton could pass under the railroad. The arches came to be well-known landmarks of our town, and the north arch was located on our street between our house and the family store. In addition to the tall railroad levee, a natural rise called Murray Hill obscured a direct view between the store and the house. The Murray family had lived there since before the Civil War.

When the alarm went off that May morning, Rudy quickly dressed and slipped out the back door, beginning the plan that my dad and several neighbors had put in place because the store had been a frequent target of thieves. Rudy quietly crept behind a row of hedges that grew along the fence west of our house. This shielded him from view if someone was on the lookout for movement at our house. The plan was for Daddy to summon the Sheriff while Rudy alerted neighbors who had offered to help in the case of an emergency. Both Mr. Olien Hindman, who lived across the street, and our cousin Otis McCalla, whose home was only two doors east of ours, had agreed in advance to shift into gear whenever necessary.

As Rudy crossed the street to alert Mr. Olien, he noticed a car sitting west of our house, near the brand new U.S. Highway 51. Suddenly, the car's headlights flashed eastward in the direction of the store! Then Rudy realized that another car, also facing east toward the store, was sitting at the top of Murray Hill. Then he saw that car also flash its lights! Now Rudy was really worried!

Rudy and the neighbors gathered at our house, and in a short time, Sheriff Scott arrived with his deputy. They stopped in the street in front of our house just long enough to gather the men and plan their advance on the store. With guns drawn, the makeshift posse, riding in our 1926 Model T Ford, traveled over Murray Hill and down through the arch, not knowing what they would find when they reached the store.

The "posse" members were shocked when they arrived. The front door was locked, and the iron bar across the two doors was in place. At first glance, nothing was amiss. As the Sheriff and Daddy peered through the windows in the top half of the doors, they were stunned. Someone had indeed been inside the store! Goods had been taken from the shelves and stacked in the aisles, ready to be hauled away. Overalls and shoes were piled on the floor. Bolts of fabric had been pulled off the shelves. A major heist had begun, but mysteriously, both the front and back doors were still barred, and the thieves were nowhere to be found.

Rudy was the first to think about looking under the store, which was built on an open foundation of stone blocks. In the corner of the store where the ground sloped away from the street, one could crawl under the building. When the summers grew hot and muggy, we children used to play in the cool, smooth dirt under the store.

Rudy followed his hunch and crawled under the building. Sure enough, he found a hole that had been cut into the floor from underneath! He poked his head up through the hole and found himself in front of Daddy's desk in the southwest corner of the store! This was where the thieves had entered and how they had made their quick escape.

Once inside, Rudy went to the back door and removed the large wooden bar to let the "posse" enter. They were flabbergasted when they saw the condition of the store. Not only were goods stacked in the aisles, but all of the candy and candy bars had been stripped from the glass shelves and strewn on the floor. Large unopened sacks of sugar had been dragged to the pile of groceries that waited to be hauled away. Paper bags of coffee had been moved to the gathering points. Stacks of canned goods towered in the aisles.

The till of the cash register had been angrily thrown to the floor. The thieves did not know the special combination of tabs and levers that caused the cash drawer to open so they had torn it out of the cash register. To their disappointment, they found that Daddy did not leave any significant amount of money in the cash register overnight. They were angry and frustrated even before they got the signal that someone was coming. Obviously, they had left in a hurry—and empty-handed.

When Daddy went to open the front doors, he found that in all of the excitement, he had left home without his keys. Rudy called the house and asked our mother, Lela, to bring the keys to the store.

In the dark of that early morning, Lela arrived bringing the keys and with me in tow. I remember her using the keys to open the tall double doors on the front and removing the heavy iron bar. I'm sure I looked like I had been dragged out of bed, which was exactly the case! After I had been awakened by the alarm and had seen everyone getting dressed, I had rolled over, buried my head under the covers, and had gone back to sleep. For years to follow, Rudy teased me about guarding the bed while the rest of the family was chasing the thieves.

As I looked around the ransacked store, I was amused to see that the thieves had apparently poured themselves a gallon jug of Rock Island Sugar House molasses. This was a delicacy that Daddy offered his customers. He was the only storekeeper in the whole area who stocked this special brand. Each September, a new barrel of this rare molasses arrived by train. Daddy and Mr. Goulder, the depot manager, would unload the barrel of Rock Island Sugar House molasses from the train and onto Daddy's wagon to be carted to the store. The barrel stood in the center aisle near the back of the store and was secured by a specially fabricated frame. The spout was turned in such a way as to permit the customers to pour their own molasses into the jugs and containers they brought with them. I remember thinking that it must have been especially frustrating for the thieves to have to run away without taking the jug of the prized molasses.

No culprits were ever charged with this burglary. We always felt that whoever was responsible knew a lot about the store, how it operated, the habits of its owners, and where we lived. They had figured out how to get into the store and where to place lookouts so that they would not get caught. Fortunately, the plan developed by my dad and our neighbors thwarted their efforts and the "posse" was able to chase them off before they could help themselves to the Rock Island Sugar House molasses and many other treasurers.

It was an exciting day for a sleepy eleven-year old girl!

Thieves by the Truckloads

Fending off thieves was a common activity in small town stores in the 1920s. On another night, a group of thieves was more successful than the ones foiled by Daddy and our neighbors. These particular burglars broke into my dad's Baird Brothers General Store and hauled away a truckload of goods.

As they were making their getaway south toward Memphis, they had a flat tire near Millington. Oddly, a friend of my dad unwittingly stopped to give them a hand. He noticed all of the "goods" in the back of the truck and asked about them. The thieves explained that they were moving, so nothing more was said.

After the tire was fixed and the thieves drove off, my dad's friend noticed one "new-looking" shoe left behind on the pavement. He picked it up and took it with him. Later, when he heard that thieves had hit the Baird Brothers General Store in Brighton, he brought the shoe to the store and asked Daddy if it looked familiar. Not only was it familiar to him, but he had the matching shoe which the thieves left behind in the shoe box! I even remember where Daddy had placed the box with the lone shoe that was left after the burglary.

Like so many other times, the thieves were never found.

Another common threat that occurred from time to time came from traveling bands of "gypsy" families. Of course, not all of these wandering Eastern Europeans caused problems, but the dishonest ones made people wary of all of them, even the honest ones. Many times these families would camp for weeks in an open field between the town and Indian Creek, just north of the Baird businesses.

From time to time, my mother, Lela, would help them when they had a special need. I remember once when a baby was born to a woman in the camp. The baby was sick and soon died. When Mother found out, she reached out with food for the family and with clothes for the baby's burial.

In spite of Lela's efforts to be a good neighbor, the general feeling was that the gypsies had to be watched. They had a reputation for shoplifting and sweeping goods into their big aprons and loose clothing when no one was looking. From time to time, an aggressive group of gypsies would pass through the area visiting a number of stores in small towns along the highway leading in and out of Memphis.

Having learned from experience with these groups of customers, storekeepers took special precautions when they learned that gypsies were in the area. Merchants in one town would call ahead to warn merchants in the next town that a band of them was coming. When gypsies came to our

General Store, Dallas Robison and Lee Smith, who worked across the street in the Baird Brothers Hardware Store, would close and lock that store and come across to the General Store so they could help Lela and JB keep an eye on the group as they shopped.

One of those warning calls came on a day when Lela was watching the store by herself. She quickly stepped onto the front porch to close and bar the doors just as a band of gypsies arrived. Two large gypsy women approached and asked to be let into the store. Mother stood firm and refused. They were angry and accused her of being a bully. To that, Mother responded that she was not a bully, but told them, "I'm bully enough to keep you out!" And she did!

A Colorful Fiasco

Paint was one of the countless products sold at the Baird Brothers stores. One day in 1929, a wholesale drummer showed up with a brand new paint product called "Nu Enamel" and wanted us to carry it in the store. His pitch to my dad was successful despite the intentional misspelling of a common word in the product's name, which was the kind of language play that really irritated my parents. The salesman convinced Daddy to allow him to demonstrate the new paint on something that everyone in town would notice —Daddy's 1926 Model T Ford!

Daddy liked the idea of a free paint job and directed the salesman to the Model T, which was parked behind the Hardware Store across the street. Pleased with the opportunity to broadly advertise his product, the Nu Enamel rep went off to show what his new product could do.

Mother had not been at the store the morning this arrangement was made. She showed up later, unaware of the sales experiment that was taking place across the street. A short time after she arrived, the salesman returned to the store and announced that the paint job was finished. He led

Daddy and Mother across the street and behind the Hardware Store to proudly demonstrate how good his "NU Enamel" product looked on the Model T.

As they rounded the corner to the spot where the car was parked, my parents were both shocked! Mother could not believe her eyes!

In an attempt to make this paint job the most effective advertisement that it could be, the drummer had used every color of Nu Enamel in his sample kit! The car was covered with geometric shapes—squares, circles, and other flashy designs—and each in a different color!

First, Mother almost fainted! Then, that petite Texas lady really blew her top! She was outraged that anyone would be so foolish as to paint an automobile in such a gaudy way. She was mad at the drummer for not explaining his plan, but she was *furious* at my dad for agreeing to the proposal without learning the details!

Of course, Daddy had not known what an unconventional car he was going to be driving after this seemingly generous sales pitch. He also could not have anticipated Mother's reaction nor could he have predicted that Mother would refuse to ride in this "clown car," as she called it!

Mother was especially serious about showing her displeasure when we went to church each Sunday. For weeks afterwards, she would walk to church, while Daddy and we kids rode by in the Nu Enamel billboard! As we sped past her, we would all wave and call to her, but she strode on briskly, pretending she did not know us.

While Daddy basically agreed with Mother's reaction, in later years, he mused that the multicolored car turned out to be a very effective advertisement. People came from everywhere to see the car folks were talking about and to buy the new brand of paint. He sold a lot of Nu Enamel that year, and even Mother finally acknowledged that "the clown car" advertisement had worked.

The Waller Kid and the Rain Barrel

Many drummers came to Daddy's store to sell their wares, but Mr. Waller from Memphis was my dad's favorite. Mr. Waller was a shoe salesman for the Peter Shoe Company, and when he came to the store, he would bring his large catalogs with photos of many different kinds of shoes. Mr. Waller also had a grand display of shoes in a large room at the opulent Gayoso Hotel in Memphis. Every time there was a change in seasons and shoe fashions, Daddy, Mother, and I would drive into Memphis to check out the new fashions for ourselves and place orders for shoes to be delivered to our store in Brighton.

When we went to Memphis to buy goods for the Baird Brothers stores, we always had several wholesalers to visit, and we would save the visit to Mr. Waller's display until last. The ride up in the elevator at the Gayoso Hotel was always a thrill, and I can still remember the rich smell of leather that greeted us on our entrance into Mr. Waller's showroom. I eventually figured out that we saved that visit to Mr. Waller until last because of what came next. Mr. Waller would close down his display room after we were finished, and he, Daddy, Mother and I would go to supper in the fancy dining room of the Gayoso. Mr. Waller would say, "Dinner is on the house!" This struck me as a funny thing to say. First of all, it was time for what we called "supper," not "dinner." Plus, I didn't know what he meant by saying that "Dinner was *on the house*." I probably never really asked about those things; I was just happy to be going to supper, or dinner, or whatever it was called.

On some trips, depending on how late it was, Mother and Daddy would decide that we should spend the night at the hotel. Daddy did not like to drive that Model T on the country roads after dark. On those evenings, we would sometimes go to the Orpheum Theater after supper to see a play. I was enchanted with the plush velvet seats and the beautiful lighted wall sconces that looked like vases of flowers with colored glass petals. I was so interested in the theater itself that I never paid much attention to the plays. After the theater, we would return to the hotel for an overnight. Mr. Waller would join us again for breakfast the next morning before we headed back to Brighton. As we parted ways with Mr. Waller, Mother would often encourage him to bring his son and come out to visit us in the country. That seemed like a wonderful idea.

During the summers, my cousin Felix Tanner would frequently spend the day with us while his mother, our Aunt Jennie, worked as a telephone operator at the exchange in Covington. This would have left Felix on his own for most summer days, so, instead, he spent most of them with us. We became great pals and playmates on those lazy summer days.

One day during the summer when I was about ten years old, Mr. Waller called to say that he was bringing his son to Brighton for a visit and to meet his "country" friends. When Mr. Waller arrived with his son, Junior, Mother brought lemonade and cookies to the front porch for refreshments. We three children—Felix, Junior, and I—quietly played games on the porch at first. As the afternoon wore on, it became apparent that Junior did not have a very high opinion about how much we "country kids" knew. He spent a lot of his time letting us know that, as a city boy, he knew a lot more than we did about quite a number of topics.

Felix and I tired of hearing all of that, and we decided that we needed a more active game. Maybe we could find *something* that we could do right. Felix suggested that we play "Annie Over." This was a chase game that involved throwing a ball over the house and into the back yard. Then the three of us would start at the small tree on the east side of the front yard, run to the back of the house, find the ball, and see who could be the first to return to the tree with the ball.

After we played this game several times, Junior, who was from the city, you know, decided that he could get to the backyard more quickly by going through the house rather than around it.

Now it was probably true that Junior, as a city boy, knew a lot of things that we did not know, but for sure he did *not know* about the Baird family's rain barrel that Mother kept next to the back porch. Mother firmly believed that rainwater got things whiter than the well water did so she captured rain in the barrel and used it for washing sheets, shirts, and tablecloths. Another plus was that any water we could easily collect in the rain barrel would be that much less that we would have to draw from the deep well. Mother kept a large piece of cloth over the top of the barrel to filter the water and keep out leaves and other trash. This large cloth was always tied around the barrel and pulled taut across the top.

As we continued to play "Annie Over," Junior took his short cut through the house. He went up the front steps, through the living room, down the hall, and out the back door. As he started to run down the back steps next to the rain barrel, he saw an opportunity to get to the back yard even more quickly by using the barrel as a springboard onto the yard. While the cloth covering kept most of the trash out of the barrel, it was not strong enough to stop Junior!

Splash!!! Kerplunk!!! Down into the barrel Junior went, up to his armpits! He fit perfectly—and Felix and I loved it!

Alerted by Junior's splashes and shouts and a few giggles from us, Mother came running with towels and apologies. The other grown-ups followed closely behind her. Everyone was concerned about poor, wet, squealing Junior, but Felix and I stood off to the side snickering quietly to ourselves. At least there was one thing that we country kids knew that Junior did not—we knew to stay off the rain barrel!

Soon afterwards, Mr. Waller took the damp and shaggy-haired Junior and left for Memphis. I don't ever recall his bringing Junior back to visit us and that was fine. Felix and I were happy to be "just us" again.

The Circus Is Coming

It sure caught my attention as I was walking home from school one afternoon. I could not believe my eyes! There on the left, just past Mr. Smithson's store, an elephant was staring right at me! He was huge! As big as the side of my family's store! Next to the elephant, there were ladies dancing, dogs jumping through hoops, and a lady with a beard smiling right at me, but I wasn't afraid. Actually, I was quite excited!

The elephant was part of a huge poster promoting the annual visit of the circus to Memphis, and it had been pasted to the side of the Baird Brothers General Store. The large outer wall of the store made a wonderful advertising space after the ice house had been moved farther back from the street. Many advertisements were posted on the store wall through the seasons, but each year's circus poster was my favorite. And I was thrilled because we were going to Memphis to see the real thing!

A few days later, there was an air of excitement as we prepared for the trip to the circus. I was not feeling too well that morning, but I did not dare tell anyone. I thought it was only my anticipation of the big day ahead. Mother had written a note to my teacher, Miss Helen Pennel (later to become Mrs. John Murray and live in the beautiful home on Murray Hill), requesting an early dismissal for me at 2:00. Mother came to school to pick up Nelle, Rudy, and me, and when we got to the store, Daddy was ready to go. We all piled into the family's Model T and headed to the Memphis Fairgrounds. As we arrived at the Fairgrounds, we parked near the place the elephants were being bathed by their trainers. I noticed that the men were using brooms to scrub the elephants, and I hoped Mother didn't get any ideas from that!

As we walked toward the big tent, we heard a man call out, "JB! JB Baird!" and a young man came running up to us. Daddy greeted him and introduced him only as "Arnold." Arnold had originally lived in Covington, but was now working for and traveling with the circus. How exciting, I thought! We were talking with someone who was actually part of the circus!

Arnold worked in a narrow wooden stand where he sold tickets. Fortunately, the JB Baird family did not have to buy tickets because ours were provided as part of the compensation that the Baird Brothers General Store received in exchange for having the circus poster pasted to the side of our building. What a deal! I loved the poster on the side of the store, *and*, on top of that, it provided admission for all of us to the circus!

I stood and listened as Daddy and Arnold talked. I learned a lot that day.

Daddy asked, "Arnold, when did you get out?"

Arnold replied, "About six months ago."

The more I listened, the more I figured out on my own that "get out" probably referred to jail or prison!

In talking about traveling with the circus, Arnold explained to Daddy how he used his job as a ticket seller to make a little extra for himself. He told Daddy that he was clever about receiving a $5 bill from a customer and quickly substituting a $1 bill for it. When the customer complained, Arnold would hold up the substituted $1 bill and insist that the customer was mistaken—later, he pocketed the other $4. He also explained how it was possible to charge a person who had requested tickets for two adults and three children for tickets for five adults. Some people had trouble with the math, and Arnold was a smooth talker. Again, he pocketed the difference at the end of the day. My dad just shook his head, and I wondered how long Arnold would "stay out" if he kept that up. As he spoke with us, someone came to relieve him for a break so he was able to walk with us and continue to share his "secrets" while adding to my "education."

As we entered the tent and looked for our free seats, we discovered that we had to climb nearly all the way to the top of the tent. Our seats were in the next to the top row Fortunately, as it turned out later, there was no one sitting in the row behind us.

Not long after we got to our seats, the music started and the parade began. I was most impressed by the entrance of the animals. They were all so well behaved. Next came the clowns. They were not well behaved! They were doing tricks, hand springs, rolling and tumbling. And they were throwing candy to the children in the audience, but none of the candy made it up to the next to the last row at the top of tent.

Soon, all three rings were abuzz with action-packed fun. The high wire walkers were making their way across the show area on a very thin wire. I remember a lady in a glittering costume riding on a camel—what a strange animal, a horse designed by a committee, they say. A troupe of dwarfs was doing special tricks and having a lot of laughs doing so. And then we got to see a real big shot—a man who was shot out of a cannon! Fortunately he landed in a net as intended, and no one was hurt.

All the while, however, I was hurting more and more. My discomfort from earlier in the day had not gone away. Instead, it was getting worse by the minute. About that time, Mother bought me a Grapette, a bottled grape drink. I downed the treat thinking it would help, but it soon came right back up! Mother saw that I was getting sick. She quickly whirled me around, grabbed my head, and directed it under the empty row of seats behind us! I was glad when that was over and really glad that the row behind us was empty.

We stayed until the circus was over, and I saw most of it, except for those times when I was looking under the seats in the row behind us. Even though I was sick, it was the best circus I ever saw.

As we left the fairgrounds, Mother bought me a gas balloon. It made me feel better for a short while as I was riding in the open back seat of our Model T. The balloon was attached by a string around my finger, but as the car increased speed and the wind picked up, the string gradually slipped off my finger. My beautiful balloon floated away! I can still see it rising higher and higher in the afternoon sky over the fairgrounds, never to be seen again…at least by us.

Each year as the circus came to Memphis, the advertising poster was pasted to the side the Baird Brothers General Store, and each year we received complimentary tickets. I always enjoyed the circus, but I never drank Grapette again!

Rudy's Cotton Crop

When my brother Rudy was sixteen years old, he decided that he needed to start making and saving money for college. He concluded that one way he could do that was to raise cotton. Of course, raising cotton was one of the most common farming activities in west Tennessee. There were cotton gins in almost every community, and the schools were closed for six weeks in the fall so the children could help bring in the cotton crops.

Daddy owned a farm on the Old Memphis Road east of Brighton. This was the road that ran from Covington to Brighton and on to Memphis. When Rudy approached Daddy with his plan to raise cotton, Daddy proposed a deal. He would allow Rudy to grow cotton on a part of that farmland and front him the start-up money he needed, *but* the money was to be considered a loan, not a gift. Rudy agreed that he would pay back the loan to Daddy, and this is how Rudy began his brief career as a cotton farmer.

First Rudy built a wagon. Using planks that he found out in our barn, he built a flat bed wagon with a small fence about one foot high around the sides and the front of the wagon.

The back of the wagon bed was open, perfect for kids to sit on and swing their legs as they rode along. On the front of the wagon, Rudy built a bench for the driver.

When we went places in the wagon with Rudy, my sister Nelle and I would usually ride on the plank floor in the back with our backs toward the driver and frequently with our feet dangling off the back of the wagon. I especially remember one evening when we had made one of our occasional trips to Mr. Marshall's farm west of Brighton. We would take our hog out to the Marshall farm for breeding, and a few days later we would go back and pick her up. We were running late one particular day and went out in the late afternoon. It grew dark as we were riding back home, and the memory of that return ride is still vivid for me. The silver moonlight was almost magical. I remember the crisp shadows cast by the moonlight and the unusual and eerie look of the landscape in that mysterious light.

Rudy was most proud of the fact that the wagon he built was a "spring wagon" and not just a plain farm wagon. I do not know where Rudy found the huge springs—perhaps our dad's hardware store—but he placed them between the axles and the wagon bed to create a smoother-riding wagon. Often, as we traveled along the road out to the farm, Rudy would ask, "Notice how smoothly my spring wagon rides?" I'm sure his wagon did bounce less than a simple farm wagon without springs, but it was difficult to compliment him on his smooth-riding wagon while we bumped along the road to the farm!

The Cullen family lived on the land that Daddy allowed
Rudy to use for his cotton farming. They worked the land for
Daddy and shared a portion of the profits from the crops
they raised. To help Rudy get started, Mr. Cullen plowed the
land and then Rudy took over. He planted the white fuzzy
cotton seeds and chopped the weeds that grew among the
cotton stalks. Most importantly, he waited and watched for
the blooms and then for the cotton bolls to form and for the
bolls to open, revealing the white fluffy cotton.

Rudy hand-picked some of the cotton himself, but the
Cullens and other farmhands picked most of it. Large cotton
wagons pulled by two horses or two mules were brought in
for the cotton-picking days. These wagons were nearly twice
as large as a regular farm wagon, and they had tall slats
around the edges with chicken wire spread from slat to slat.
There was a long arm on the back of the wagon where Rudy
would hang the cotton scales. Each farmhand would bring
his bagful of cotton to the wagon and weigh its content. This
was important for keeping track of what each farmhand had
earned that day. They were paid one penny per pound of
picked cotton. Weighing the cotton was also important for
deciding when the wagon was full enough to head to the gin.

My sister Nelle, who was fourteen at the time, and I would
often go out to the farm with Rudy as he "played" farmer.
The Cullens were a very pleasant and friendly black family.
In addition to Mr. Cullen, there was his wife, Belle, and two
children about my age. My strongest memory is of the son
everybody called "Sugar Cat." Belle was a wonderful
housekeeper and an even greater cook. She always made

Rudy, Nelle, and me feel very welcome and like a part of their family.

Each day that we went to the farm, the Baird Brothers General Store provided our lunches. We would help ourselves to Vienna sausages, potted meat, sardines, lots of cookies and candy, and bottled drinks. When it came to be lunchtime, Sugar Cat was more interested in what we had brought from the store instead of the wonderful food his mother had prepared. I was very eager to hand over my lunch from the store to Sugar Cat for an opportunity to sit at the Cullen's table and enjoy Belle's wonderful cooking.

While Rudy worked in the field, Nelle and I played with the Cullen children. Since Nelle was a few years older than the rest of us, she appointed herself the "boss." As it often goes with older siblings, we pretty much did what she said we should do.

We three Baird kids were expected to be home before sundown. Eventually, Rudy would look at the position of the sun, estimate the time of day, and announce that it was "quitting time" and time to head for home. When we got back to Brighton, we stopped at the store and let Daddy know that we were home.

I don't remember how Rudy made out with his cotton crop or how long he stayed with it or even if he paid back the original loan to Daddy. Knowing Rudy, I'm sure he did. In addition to what he made toward his college fund, he also made some pretty wonderful memories for me.

Bones

During the years of the Great Depression, being a storeowner was both good news and bad. Many businesses closed completely, and people lost their jobs. The banks failed, and if people had money in a bank, they were not able to withdraw it. Money was tight, yet people still needed to buy food, clothing, and all of the necessities. Sometimes they found creative ways to pay their debts, ways that storeowners' kids found more interesting than did the storeowners themselves.

Many people were not able to pay their debts during those difficult years. Daddy carried people on credit as long as he could, but eventually they had to "settle up" somehow. He was agreeable to many non-monetary ways that people found to pay their bills. I got my first car as a result of a customer settling his debt with the General Store by turning over his Model A Ford Coupe. Since Daddy was unable to sell the car, he kept it and used it for a while. As he and Mother tired of driving me to school, he suggested I drive myself using the Ford coupe. In 1931, I was the only student driving her own car to Brighton High School! The law said you had to be sixteen years old to drive, and I was a fourteen-year-old freshman at the time. I drove that car for two whole years before Daddy was able to sell it.

Another time, a business man from Mississippi who had borrowed money from Daddy was having trouble paying what he owed because his cash had been frozen. This man was involved in a business that used horses and mules. He told daddy that the only way he could pay his debt was in animals from his farm. Daddy was not happy about it, but what else could he do? *And Mother was even unhappier about it!*

When the animals showed up, they looked pitiful. They were just skin and bones. They had not been fed well, and it showed. They were brought to our barn and housed in the barn lot behind our house. We had to draw water from our well for them, and their food was taken from sacks of horse feed for sale at our Baird Hardware Store. After a long time of caring for them, Mother finally declared, "These animals are going to the "Onion Farm"!

The "Onion Farm " was our family's nickname for a patch of land about one mile south of town. The Baird Brothers owned it and had it farmed, but it was not especially productive. Daddy used to say that the only thing that grew out there was wild onions, and that's how it came to be called the "Onion Farm."

In preparation for the new animals, Daddy had to secure help and supplies to patch the bad places in the fence at the farm. While all the preparations were taking place to move the Mississippi animals to the "Onion Farm," I was becoming more and more attached to one particular horse. I fell in love with a skinny white horse who had a bald spot on his hip where no hair grew. Mr. Lee Smith, an older gentleman who worked at the hardware store, had suggested that I rub that spot with medicated Vaseline, which, of course, I got from the store. That was not the answer, and the bald patch on my horse never grew hair.

When all of the other animals went to the Onion Farm, I was allowed to keep that horse in our barn for a while longer. I had named him "Bones" because he was just skin and bones. He and I became quite good friends. He allowed me to grab his mane and use it to pull him in whatever direction I wanted him to go.

As long as I rode Bones and looked after him, Daddy allowed me to keep him at the barn in our back yard. When I stopped paying as much attention to him, he was taken to join his Mississippi cousins out on the Onion Farm.

I still maintained my interest in Bones even though riding him became more complicated. Daddy kept the bridle and saddle at the store. I would walk over to the store and pick up the bridle. I would then walk out to the Onion Farm on my own and whistle for Bones. He always responded like a big dog and walked right up to me. He would lower his head and allow me to put the bridle on him. I would then lead him to the nearest tree stump. I would get up on the stump and, with the extra height it provided, I would pull myself up on Bones' back while holding on to his mane.

Once I was up on Bones' back, I would ride bare-back into town to the General Store. There Daddy would help me put the saddle on Bones, and I would ride around Brighton and out into the adjacent farm areas. When I was done, I had to reverse the process—ride back to the store, leave the saddle with Daddy, ride bare-back to the Onion Farm, and then walk back into town. Eventually, Mother decided that it was too dangerous for me to walk back and forth to the farm on my own so she would drive me out to the farm and then bring me home when I had finished riding. While this worked out fine, it meant that I was no longer able to come and go on my own. I could only go when Mother would be able to drive me.

This routine went on for several years as my friendship with Bones grew. He was never a beautiful animal, but he was beautiful to me. He was a true friend. By the time I got to high school, I spent less and less time with him. Finally, it was time to say good-bye to Bones. Daddy arranged for a man who lived near Brighton to take care of him. This man offered to let me come out and ride Bones whenever I wanted. I never took him up his offer, but every time I saw this new owner, he assured me that Bones was doing fine. I always wondered if he missed me as much as I missed him.

Rudy's Best Mistake

During the crisis years of the Great Depression, many Brighton families struggled as did families throughout the country. There were huge "runs" on banks in the fall of 1930 and into the next four years. These caused banks all across the nation to close, and no one could get to their money at all. People with money in the bank were caught "short" — and lost all the funds they had in the banks. I kept hearing people say that their money was "frozen," but as a child, I did not really understand what that meant. I just knew it was serious.

Conditions for our family were not as bad as things were for many because Daddy had a lot of goods in the store and not many customers with money to buy them. Therefore, our family did not feel the same tight pinch because we had access to what we needed through the store.

Everyday in the late afternoon, our father would tally the day's income, bundle it up, and take it to the bank. Frequently, my brother Rudy would help Daddy by taking the day's deposit to the bank for him since the bank was just around the corner from the General Store.

One day, in the early 1930s, Daddy had asked him to take the day's income to the bank at the end of the day. That afternoon, Rudy and his good friend Leroy Hindman got busy talking and planning their evening's activities. Rudy let the time get away from him and missed the end of the bank's business day. The deposit did not make it to the bank!

Daddy was none too happy at the time, but his upset turned to relief when the next day dawned, and we learned that the banks had failed and would not reopen. No one could retrieve their savings! If Rudy had deposited that money, it would have been lost! As a result of Rudy's "mistake," the store's income was not frozen and our family had a little extra cash to see us through the tough times at the beginning of the Great Depression.

For many years, our dad would joke and say, "Rudy forgot to do what he was supposed to do, and it was the best thing he ever did."

Brighton, Tennessee, c. 1920

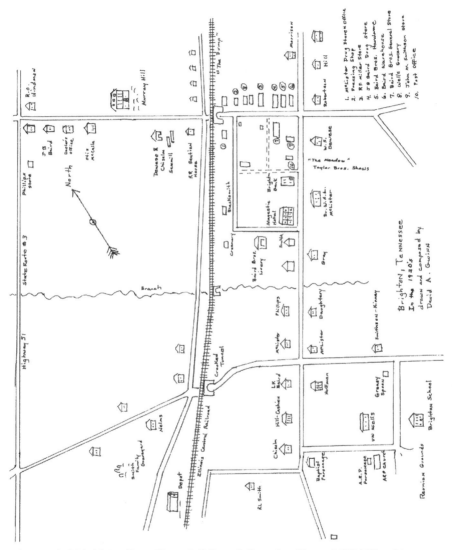

Legend: 1.McLister Drug Store & Office; 2.Pressing Shop; 3.RF Miller Store; 4.JB Baird Drug Store; 5.Baird Bros Hardware; 6.Baird Warehouse; 7.Baird Bros General Store; 8.Wells Grocery; 9.John M. Smithson Store; 10.Post Office

Map courtesy of David A. Gwinn

Part Three
Life in Brighton as We Knew It

Brighton High School, Brighton, Tennessee.

Taylor Brothers Show

Every summer during the 1920s, the traveling "Taylor Brothers Show" would come to Brighton. They would set up a huge tent in the meadow that was located between the DeWese home and Dr. Billy McLister's home across the street from the Majestic Hotel. As if the large tent weren't enough of a curiosity, they also strung the tent with electric lights powered by a generator that they brought with them. At that time, the only electric lights in Brighton were in the Baird Brothers stores and Smithson's grocery store. I still remember the bright lights and the noise of the generator that kept them glowing.

We children were really excited to see the tent going up because we knew it meant a week of outdoor entertainment. Many of the adults were excited, too. The tent stood for a week, and every night people would gather for a show that included movies as well as all kinds of live entertainment. It was usually introduced by Washington Didonia Elihu Davis, a multi-talented black man who was the focus of the show. He was the Master of Ceremonies and a wonderful dancer. The individual acts included a variety of singing, comedy, and dancing.

In the middle of the show, salesmen made pitches for their products. I especially remember the night a jewelry salesman peddled engraved rings and offered to engrave them on site. Throughout the show, the audience was encouraged to buy boxes of popcorn. Each box contained a prize. Members of the audience were asked to tell what prizes they found in their boxes. Sometimes they were wonderful prizes of significant value. More often they were trinkets, such as small toys or whistles. The mix was just enough to keep the audience buying boxes of popcorn and hoping for a nice prize.

Each night, the highlight came when Washington Didonia Elihu Davis opened a prize box for all to witness. The suspense built… With great fanfare, he reached inside and found this purple piece of silk. Hand over hand, he slowly pulled it out of the box. He pulled and pulled, but the cloth just kept coming. When he finally pulled it all out, he held it up and the crowd roared at the largest pair of purple underpants they had ever seen!

One year, our nanny, Grace Fayne, fell in love with Washington Didonia Elihu Davis. They were married by Grace's father, who was the preacher at one of the local churches. When the tents were taken down and the show moved on to the next stop, Grace went with them. We were all very sad to see her leave. However, in less than a year, Grace came back to Brighton. We welcomed her home, and she remained an important part of our family for many years to come. And so did our recollections of The Taylor Brothers Show!

The DeWese and Chisolm Sawmill

As I look back on my childhood days in Brighton, I am always pleased to remember how self-sufficient our community was and how so much of what we needed was right there in town. In this context, I fondly remember the DeWese-Chisolm Sawmill.

The sawmill was owned by Mr. John Chisolm and Mr. Walter DeWese. It was located on the same street on which we lived and was between our house and the railroad. It was on the south side of the street now called Woodlawn, and across from the two-story Victorian house where the Murrays lived.

I passed by the sawmill frequently on my walk to Daddy's store. I would also have to pass it when I was walking to and from school. I was fascinated by the operation of the sawmill, and I always had a desire to go over and watch the men unload the logs as they arrived. I also enjoyed watching the sharp and noisy blade slice the logs into planks or boards. I especially loved the "sweet aroma" of the sawdust. Even today, I can close my eyes and remember that fragrant smell. Perhaps this was the beginning of my lifelong love of wood and working with wood.

I also loved the shrill sound of the sawmill whistle. It is one of my favorite memories of Brighton. The whistle was blown four times a day: in the morning; at Noon to signal the beginning of the lunch hour; at 1:00 to mark the end of the lunch hour; and at 5:00, the close of the work day. I was so fascinated with the whistle that I would frequently ask to be allowed to blow it. I would run over to the sawmill just before 5:00. The men let me climb up on "the stump," which was a block formed by a part of a log so I could pull the whistle right at 5:00 P.M. What a thrill that was for me! I must have been the peskiest kid in Brighton.

I have a clear memory of Mr. Johnson McLelland driving a large wagon that he frequently used to haul logs to the sawmill. Because he often had to drag his load of logs out of very muddy areas, he covered the sides of the wheels with solid sheets of wood so the mud would not clog up the wagon's spokes. He also "single-handedly" handled a team of six or seven horses in spite of having lost part of his left arm, just below the elbow. He called that arm his "stump," and he frequently held it high in the air as he drove the team.

Mr. McLelland, who was a teamster at a logging camp, would ride on one of the six horses, which were teamed together in front of the huge wagon. Usually the horse he rode was the only white horse in the group. Occasionally, a seventh horse, which was usually white, was harnessed at the head of the team. Mr. McLelland draped the lines for all of the horses across the stump of his arm, and he held a whip in his right hand. If one of the horses was "playing lazy," as he would say, he would give that horse a "touch" with the end of the whip. Sometimes he would reach for one of the leads draped across his stump and give a slight pull to a horse that was beginning to "slack." The "slack horse" realized that if he did not respond to this gentle tug, a sharper message would soon come from the whip. It was fascinating to watch this man and his team of six or seven horses maneuver that large wagon loaded with heavy logs through our little town. It was an entertaining sight!

After logs were unloaded at the sawmill, they were cut into planks or boards and loaded onto a rail cart. When the cart was full, it was pushed on a small set of rails down the hill toward the railroad line and unloaded onto rail cars for delivery to the buyers of the cut lumber. Planks that were not yet ready to be shipped were arranged in stacks that we called "pig pens" where they waited until the entire shipment was ready to go.

The children in the neighborhood enjoyed playing at the sawmill after it closed. We especially liked to push the empty rail car across the flat part of the mill's property and toward the hill that led down toward the railroad tracks. As the cart approached the downhill stretch, the pushers would quickly hop on, joining the others who were already on board, and we would all enjoy the fast ride down toward the tracks. At the bottom of the hill, there was a slight upgrade as the track began to rise toward the rail line. This grade would stop the momentum of the cart. Then we would all get off and push it back up the hill toward the sawmill. This uphill push was a lot of work, but the thrill of the ride down the hill made it all worthwhile!

Brighton's Majestic Hotel

When I was growing up in the 1920s, there were only two buildings in Brighton that had more than one story. One was the Baird Brothers Hardware and the other was one of my favorite places, the Majestic Hotel. How I loved to go there!

My family had a close friendship with the J.C. McLister family who had built and first operated the Majestic. At the time I was growing up, the hotel was run by Mr. McLister's grandson, "Joe" (Norman E. Smith), and his wife Nora Huffman Smith. The Smith family's daughter, Florene, was a couple years older than I was, and playing with Florene gave me an excuse for dropping into the hotel on a regular basis.

From time to time, my family would go to the Majestic for supper. "Miss" Nora was a terrific cook! I vividly remember dining at the long, long table in the center of the dining room. Many people could sit at this table for a meal, and in the center of it was the largest Lazy Susan I have ever seen in my life! From this rotating server, we could choose from many bowls of food, all piled high with the most wonderful tasting selections you can imagine. People sitting at the center of the table could reach the bowls they wanted as the Lazy Susan swung *lazily* around, but the diners sitting at the ends of the long table had to ask the folks in the center to pass the bowls of food. Going to the Majestic for supper was one of the best treats of my childhood!

Actually, merely entering the Majestic was thrilling for me. The two-story building had two porches on the front—one on each level. Guests would sit in rocking chairs on the lower level porch, and occasionally, when the porches were empty and we would not disturb the guests, Florene and I would play on the upper porch. Inside the front door of the hotel was a lobby with several large brown chairs and a grand staircase with a newel post that I remember touching every time I passed it.

The most fascinating part of the Majestic for me was a "cage" that stood in the right-hand corner of the lobby. It had a small window, and the window had bars on it. How strange, I thought! It was a mystery because I could see no door into the cage. There was usually someone in there, but they didn't seem to mind. I could not help staring at that cage as I wondered about it. Eventually, I found out that the cage was called the cashier's window, and the cashier voluntarily got into and out of it through a door that entered this tiny office through a larger office behind it.

While playing around the hotel, I got to meet and make friends with some of the regular guests. One of my favorites was Jess Moore, a jolly drummer who often came to Brighton. I first met Jess when he would come to Daddy's store selling his wholesale wares. He was always kind to me, just a little girl playing in her family's store.

In the evenings after their days of selling, traveling salesmen would stay at the comfortable and pleasant Majestic Hotel. After a fine meal cooked by Miss Nora, there would be music and dancing and socializing. It was quite a place! My friend Jess played the piano and danced—in fact, he was known as the "dancing fool"! And he didn't seem to mind the title! As a child, I could hardly wait for Jess to come to town every few months.

Another group that came to the Majestic each year was the Chautauqua troop. They stayed in town for a week, putting on a show each night, with singing, dancing, plays, and lectures. People noticed that Jess would always come to Brighton during the week that the Chautauqua was in town. That may have had something to do with another friend of mine, Irene Dean, who traveled with the Chautauqua troop. Both Jess and Irene became good friends of mine, even though I was just a kid, and soon we noticed that they were good friends with each other, too!

I can still remember my excitement the day that Irene and Jess told me that they were going to be married. I grew even more excited when I learned that the wedding was going to be at the Majestic! Then something marvelous took place… *they asked me to be in their wedding! I thought I would faint!*

When Irene and Jess asked me to carry the bride's train in their wedding, I quickly agreed—and then I wondered: "What do they mean by the bride's *train*?" The only train I knew roared through Brighton several times a day and occasionally stopped to drop off goods and passengers and *The Covington Leader,* Tipton County's weekly newspaper. "How was I going to carry a train?" I wondered. Apparently, I looked confused because Irene explained what I would do in the wedding and that she was sure I could handle it.

I ran out the door of the hotel, racing down the block and around the corner to Daddy's store. I couldn't wait to ask Mother if I could be in the wedding and carry Irene's train! I charged into the store and blurted out, "Mr. Jess and Miss Irene are going to get married!"

Puzzled, Mother and Daddy asked me, "Are you telling the truth? We haven't heard anything about Jess and Irene getting married…"

I jumped up and down and squealed, "Its true; it's true! And Irene even asked me to be in the wedding and carry her train!" Of course, Mother and Daddy gave their approval, and they both enjoyed my happiness for my friends and for myself.

Now came the difficult part. I had to wait for the wedding until Jess and Irene returned to Brighton. It seemed like forever.

Finally the wedding day came. The Majestic Hotel was bustling with excitement. I was wearing a new white dress and shiny black patent leather slippers fresh from Daddy's store. As the guests began to arrive, I was sent upstairs to wait for the bride. As usual, I rubbed the newel post at the bottom of the stairs as I passed. I found a bench in the upstairs hallway where I sat and waited. I could hear the buzz of excited people downstairs, and I listened quietly as it grew to a low roar. Then someone started playing the piano. I remember wondering if it was Jess on the keyboard.

About that time, Irene came out of one of the hotel rooms. She was beautiful! I was in awe of her glowing face and beautiful white dress. We had been told to stay upstairs until we heard the piano play "Here Comes the Bride." When we heard those familiar chords, we moved toward the staircase. Irene first thought that perhaps she could allow the train to naturally follow her down the stairs. The other lady who was with us, the Maid of Honor I guess, said, "I think it would be better if you let Vivian pick it up and follow you down." I felt like such an important part of the ceremony!

As we started down the staircase, the eyes of all the guests were on the three of us—the bride, her attendant, and me. Perhaps they were looking at the bride more than the two who were carrying the train, but I felt very honored. When we got to the lobby, Irene turned and walked to the back of the large room where the Preacher was waiting. And there was Jess, looking so very handsome in his dark suit and his big smile. When Irene walked up to the Preacher, the Maid of Honor and I gently laid the train in a neat fan shape on the floor. We then stepped back and stood near the end of the train where we stayed for the rest of the ceremony.

The lobby, filled with guests, was standing room only. Friends stood around the walls surrounding the bride and groom. It seemed to me like a huge crowd. After the wedding, there was a wonderful party for all of the guests. As it was winding down, Jess and Irene Moore made their way to the train station and took the evening train out of Brighton for their honeymoon. I went home as a very happy little girl.

Jess and Irene remained my good friends for many years as I grew up. I was always grateful for the wonderful memories they gave me, which have lasted my lifetime as have my fond recollections of Brighton's lovely Majestic Hotel.

A Saturday Shooting in Brighton

Every summer, our Brighton Associate Reformed Presbyterian Church held a week-long revival meeting. This was a special occasion in our small town and usually involved a guest minister from a distant congregation. Mother and Daddy always attended, and they took me with them to the evening services every night for the whole week.

On the last night of a revival week when I was about seven years old, Mother allowed me to sit alone in the balcony, which I regarded as a real treat. She arranged for me to sit in the front row of the balcony facing the raised choir loft where she would be sitting. This put me at the eye level of the choir and permitted her to keep an eye on me and my behavior while she sang.

Without warning, just as that evening's service was about to end, a white wave entered the sanctuary and moved quietly down the center aisle. The sinister wave was created by eight or ten men dressed in long white sheets with their heads and faces completely covered by white hoods. The minister and the entire congregation were shocked into silence!

The cloaked men lined up across the front of the church. One of them spoke to the congregation. I don't remember what he said, but I do recall that when he finished, he turned and placed an envelope on the altar. Then, as ominously as it had entered, the white wave moved quietly back down the aisle and out the front door.

When we got home after the service, the disturbing visit from what I learned was the Ku Klux Klan was the talk of our family and neighbors. Everyone wondered about the menacing figures and why they left an envelope filled with money. No one seemed to know who was under those cloaks and hoods, although most had their suspicions.

I spoke up and said, "I know who *one* of them was."

At that, my daddy probed, "How do you know? They all had their faces covered."

I replied, "I could tell that one of them was Mr. Smithson. His legs bow backwards, just like mine do. I see them when he comes into our store so I could tell that was him by the way his sheet hung down on his bow legs."

No one commented on my observation at the time, but I got the sense that Daddy and the others knew I was on to something.

And as time unfolded, things confirmed that I was right.

It wasn't long after the white wave incident at our church that I got further confirmation of how Mr. Smithson felt about our African American neighbors.

Every year, the "old soldiers reunion" for veterans of the Civil War was held in Brighton on the school grounds and on adjoining land that was owned by the Baird Brothers. This was a well-attended event that attracted people from far away and required extra trains to be put on the line to bring all those people to our little town.

Also, every year, the black people of our town and surrounding communities held a large picnic on the same grounds the day after the old soldiers' reunion. It, too, drew a big crowd.

One year the driver of the Coke-a-Cola truck approached Mr. Smithson because he was concerned about making a delivery to the black people's picnic. Mr. Smithson, who was some kind of peace officer for the town, agreed to accompany the driver to the picnic grounds and jumped on the running board of the truck.

As they approached the picnic grounds, Mr. Bob Hall who worked at the "pressing shop," a barber shop that local black people frequented, was apparently blocking the way for the "Coke" truck to enter. Mr. Smithson spoke harshly to Mr. Hall and hollered to him, "Get out of the way, N.....!" Mr. Hall reportedly cursed Mr. Smithson before moving out of the way.

But the matter did not end there.

The next day, I was playing with friends on the porch of the DeWese home, which faced my family's General Store and Mr. Smithson's dry goods store. My playmate Helen DeWese and I were riding in the front-porch swing. My sister Nelle and Helen's sisters Alene and Kathryn were sitting on the edge of the porch with their legs swinging down. We all saw Mr. Smithson walk out of his grocery store and go behind

Daddy's general store, heading west toward the barber shop, which was located near the railroad tracks. We continued to play until, suddenly, we all heard one very loud gun shot!

We did not know where the shot came from or what had happened. A moment later, we did see Mr. Smithson walking quickly away from the shop, back toward his store, with his head down and carrying a pistol. Then we noticed a stream of people running toward the barber shop—all except my mother who came running toward the DeWese home to make sure that we were alright.

The people who ran to the barber shop found Bob Hall dead with one bullet to the head. Many people swarmed around the barber shop buzzing about what had happened. The town constable and the Sheriff showed up. Everyone seemed to know that Mr. Smithson had shot Mr. Hall.

Repulsed and sickened by this senseless killing, my daddy confronted Mr. Smithson who retorted, "He'll never curse me again."

I seem to remember that Mr. Smithson was arrested and tried, but not convicted. Some don't remember there ever being a trial.

Whatever the judicial result, a life was violently taken in a shameful and hateful act that certainly should have been punished.

High Stakes in Brighton

It may surprise you to learn that when I was a youngster in the 1920s, there was gambling right there in our neighborhood in the quiet little town of Brighton. It did not seem unusual to us because we grew up with it, and we loved it! Here's how my gambling career began—and ended.

Many days when I was in the eighth and ninth grades, I would walk home from school with my friend Nell Hindman. She was a year or two ahead of me in school and lived across the street. Our route took us past my family's General Store where I would stop in to let my folks know that school was over and I was on my way home. My parents probably would have been shocked to realize that on many days I would stop at their cash register, move the cash drawer, and find the canvas sack where Daddy kept the extra coins. I would open the sack with its leather tie and casually help myself to a handful of nickels.

After dropping my books off at home, I would cross the street and holler for my friend Nell. We would make our way to Phillips Grocery Store and Restaurant located on Rt. 51, south of our street and just a few minutes from our homes.

There were two big attractions at the Phillips's store—penny candy, but more importantly, a slot machine!

Nell and I made a habit of going there after school, and we just loved to try our luck! Occasionally, we would win small amounts at the slot machine, but we never hit the big jackpot. Mr. Clarence Phillips and his wife, Miss Lyde, turned their backs to the fact that these two young girls were regular visitors to their candy counter *and* their slot machine.

The Phillips's store also had a special game that combined our fondness of candy and the fun of gambling. There was a certain kind of candy that was a gamble—if the piece you selected had a colored center, you were eligible for a prize! The amount of the prize was determined by the color inside the candy. Of course, most of the time it was white on the inside, which meant no prize.

We would each buy a piece of that candy and eagerly break it open to see if we won anything. One day I selected a piece that had a pink center. To my glee, this made me eligible for a $5 gold piece! I was overjoyed and raced to cash in, but Mrs. Phillips explained that, unfortunately, they did not have any gold pieces, so she would have to pay me with five $1 bills. While I was happy to have won $5, I was really disappointed that I did not get the valuable gold piece that was promised.

In my upset, I made the mistake of heading to my folks' general store to complain to my mother. And was she ever astonished! First of all, she was appalled to learn that her young daughter was gambling after school. Secondly, she shared my dismay that Mr. and Mrs. Phillips did not deliver what was promised.

Mother promptly removed her apron and made her way directly to the Phillips's store to lodge our complaint. Mrs. Phillips explained that they did not have the gold pieces to give out and that paying with the five $1 bills was the best that they could do. Mother spoke her mind to Mrs. Phillips, pointing to the sign on the counter that clearly said "Pink-centered pieces receive a $5 gold piece." It did no good.

Although Mother understood my disappointment, she firmly let me know that my slot-playing days were over—as were my after-school trips to gamble at Phillips Grocery Store and Restaurant!

Picking Up the Covington Leader

The Illinois Central Railroad plays a big part in my childhood memories. Early every Thursday evening, a train approaching Brighton from the north would sound its loud whistle at 6:14 P.M. sharp. This was the signal for many of the children of Brighton to head for the post office. On Thursdays, this particular train brought *The Covington Leader,* our county's weekly newspaper, and it was a special event for the town.

As the train was pulling into the station, Mr. John Banks, the town barber who also worked for the Post Office, would head to the train station to pick up the mail and copies of *The Covington Leader.* In the meantime, many of us children would crowd into the main room of the Post Office. As we waited for Mr. Banks to bring the mail and newspapers, we kept our eager eyes on the wooden shutter that was closed across the Post Office service window. Mr. Cliff Phillips, the husband of Miss Mamie D. Phillips, the Post Mistress, would mingle with the children and terrorize us by pulling our ears. That made us even happier when, at last, we would hear the familiar "click, click, click" of the shutter when Miss Mamie opened up the service window.

As the children moved toward the window, Mr. Cliff made certain that all was orderly. As each child got to the window to pick up his or her family's copy of *"The Leader"* as it was commonly called, Miss Mamie would recognize each one and call us by name. She would also give us any mail for our families that had not been picked up earlier in the day.

I remember being baffled at this, and one day I asked Daddy with amazement, "How does Miss Mamie know my name?"

Calling me by my nickname, Daddy assured me, "That's her job, Billie."

I would always take the mail and *The Leader* to my Daddy at the store. First, he would take a look to see what had arrived, then each time, he would tell me the same thing: "Take it to the house, Billie," which I did.

On Thursday evenings, like many of the children in Brighton, I looked forward to Daddy reading me the cartoons in the paper that had just arrived. When the day was winding down, I would curl up in his lap while he read me the adventures of "Uncle Wiggly" and "Nurse Jane Fuzzy-Wuzzy," and all was right with the world.

Radio Comes to Brighton

In the mid-1920s, when I was about ten years old, exciting news traveled around Brighton—three families had purchased radios! In addition to the Nelms family and Leno Morrison, my brother Rudy was one of the first in our town to own a radio. Until the early 1920s, radios were not available for purchase by civilians. The models at that time were crystal radios, which ran on batteries. It was a good thing they did, because we did not yet have electricity in Brighton!

I remember the day Rudy brought his crystal radio into the General Store and assembled it. The main unit of the radio was a structure that was about the size of a tin can. It was eight inches tall and four inches in diameter. There was a socket on the bottom of this unit. I remember Rudy putting together the three-legged stand which he then screwed into the socket on the base of the radio. The radio would stand on this tripod, but it never looked very stable. On top of the unit was a small crystal about the size of a dime. Two thin wands were attached to the sides of the unit. As I remember it, these wands could be moved and adjusted over the top of the crystal. One wand was responsible for capturing the radio waves that were sent out by the radio station's broadcasting system. The other was adjusted to strengthen and clarify the signal.

The radio also had two sets of headphones. Wires that came from the side of the unit fed into these headphones. Since there was no speaker or amplifier, the headphones were the only way that a person could listen so only two people at a time could hear what was being picked up by this new invention. We found it incredible to hear what was being broadcast, whether music or speeches or boxing matches!

As more and more people stopped by our house to hear this amazing new invention, my mother, Mama Lela, decided to try a way of magnifying the sound from the headphones so that more than two people could listen. She placed a large glass bowl on the table next to the radio and then placed both sets of headphones in the bowl. Anyone who could get his or her ear close enough to the bowl could dimly hear what was coming out of the earphones. This allowed more people to listen to the radio at the same time, although it did require an awkward posture and a little contorting to get your ear close to the glass bowl!

Rudy's second radio was slightly larger than the first, and it could accommodate four sets of headphones. It was more powerful, and we could hear it more clearly. Radio was still a novelty, and friends continued to come over so they could experience it for themselves!

Soon Brighton got electricity, and Daddy ended up with a large console radio. My sister Nelle and her husband, H.B.

McCain, had purchased the console radio for their first apartment, which was in Covington where they had electricity. When they bought a house in Idaville, near H.B.'s family, they were back to living without electricity so they sold their new console radio to our dad.

That large console radio became quite an attraction in Brighton, especially as the date for a very popular prize fight approached. So many people asked JB and Lela about stopping over to listen to the fight on the radio that they needed to come up with a way of accommodating them all. Lela had JB bring the radio out on to the front porch of the house and run the electric cord through the window. She then rounded up as many chairs as we could find, lined them up on the front lawn, and invited neighbors over to listen to the fight. After the fight was over, she served refreshments to all who attended.

At the same time this new invention brought the news of the world to our small town, it also brought our town together in a new and entertaining way.

Driving The Gulf Limited

Mr. Leno Morrison and his wife, Miss Mildred, lived near Daddy's General Store on Brighton's main drag, the street now called Woodlawn. There was a barber shop just west of our store, then an open lot, and then the Morrison's pretty white house. Mr. Leno, as we all called him, was the Gulf Oil distributor in our area and had an office in Covington. Nearly everyday, Mr. Leno would drive his gas tanker to Memphis, fill its giant tank with gasoline, and bring it back to the depot in Covington. From there, the gas would be taken by smaller trucks to the service stations in the area.

When it came time for me to go to college in 1935, I chose to stay close to home rather than follow my brother and sister to Bryson College, which was 250 miles east in Fayetteville, Tennessee. Instead, I enrolled at the State Teachers' College in Memphis. I lived in a dorm at school during the week, but I came home every weekend. Why? My boyfriend Winfield "Bill" McLennan! Bill who eventually became my husband, was the primary reason I wanted to be able to get back home to Brighton every weekend.

I also wanted to stay home for Sunday evenings so I could be with Bill as much as possible, but I did not think I would be able to get to Monday morning classes on time if I did. Finally, I thought of Mr. Leno! One weekend while I was home, I asked him if I could ride into Memphis with him on Monday mornings, and he said he would be happy to have the company. Yay! I now had an opportunity to spend three nights at home each weekend!

On Monday mornings, we could depend on hearing the rumble of Mr. Leno's truck when he revved up the engine. The Morrison home was about two long blocks east of our house, but the noise of his truck starting up could be heard all the way up the hill. When we heard the truck start up, Mother and I would walk down the hill to the end of our driveway. Soon Mr. Leno would come up the hill and stop to pick me up. On these rides to Memphis, I named his truck the "Gulf Limited." What an elegant way for a young co-ed to go off to college!

It was difficult for me to reach the high step to get into the cab, and once there, I had to hang on for dear life because there were no seat belts at that time. Once we got to Memphis, Mr. Leno would drop me off where I could catch a streetcar to take me to the campus, which was east of downtown Memphis. After I got off the streetcar, I would then walk a couple blocks to my dormitory. It was a complicated journey, but, as I said, it allowed me to spend an extra evening with Bill.

Occasionally, my friend Helen DeWese would ride with us into Memphis on Monday morning. Sometimes we were also able to hitch a ride home on the "Gulf Limited" on Fridays. On those days, Helen and I would take a street car from the campus to Front Street on the high bluff above the Mississippi River. There we would perch on the benches behind Bry's Department Store and wait for Mr. Leno. Eventually, the "Gulf Limited" would arrive, and we would get on board for the trip home to Brighton.

The more experience Helen and I had riding in the tanker, the more we wondered if we might be able to drive it ourselves. Mr. Leno thought that was a good idea, and he offered to teach us. First, we practiced driving it around the depot in Covington. He taught us how to start and stop the truck and to make the wide turns necessary to maneuver that big thing. He also taught us how to go in reverse and to pull in beside a platform. As our ability to handle the truck improved, Mr. Leno let us do a little driving around Brighton. I remember one day pulling away from the Morrison house, passing Daddy's store on the right, turning and driving down the main street past the Majestic Hotel, then turning toward Brighton School, making circles in the school's big parking lot, leaving there and driving past Brighton Presbyterian Church, and then heading back toward the Morrison house. By then, Mr. Leno felt that both Helen and I were able to handle the truck effectively. We enjoyed the experience, but we never thought that it would come in handy. We just thought it was fun!

One Monday morning on our journey back to college, Mr. Leno told us that he and his wife Miss Mildred, had an appointment in Memphis the following Friday. He asked if Helen and I could help him out by driving the truck back to

Brighton so that he could go to the appointment with his wife and then ride home with her in her car. We were rather surprised at his request and his trust, but he insisted that we could handle it, so we agreed.

Just as usual, we were supposed to meet Mr. Leno and Miss Mildred behind Bry's at 3:00 P.M. on that Friday. Early that morning, however, Helen realized that she had a conflict. Her job on campus was to play the piano for Physical Education classes, and she was scheduled for a class that afternoon at the same time we were supposed to meet Mr. Leno! Of course, we were unable to get in touch with him in advance, so I went ahead with the plan to meet him and Miss Mildred behind Bry's at 3:00.

When I showed up at the meeting place, Mr. Leno had not yet arrived, but Miss Mildred was already there. When I told her that Helen was not able to join me, she became very upset. I guess she was not confident that I could handle the truck by myself. She was more comfortable with the plan when she thought that Helen, who was a college Senior, would be the driver. She did not appear to have the same confidence in me, a 5'1" Freshman.

When Mr. Leno arrived and I explained the predicament, he very calmly said, "That's all right, Bill. You can handle it." He trustingly handed me the keys, but I do not recall what Miss Mildred said about that. I was too preoccupied with fright about this big responsibility. *"Could I really do this?"*

Mr. Leno explained that he had confidence in me. "You know the way to Brighton so you won't get lost, and you know how to drive the tanker. When you get to Brighton, park the truck in front of my house and leave the keys in it."

My heart was pounding! I did not think I could do it, but I didn't have another option.

I got behind the wheel, started that noisy engine, and cautiously pulled off from where the truck was parked along Front Street. With a lump in my throat and a tight grip on the wheel, I made it all the way to Brighton without incident. Whew! I was home! I couldn't believe it—the thirty-five-mile trip was easy, and there was no trouble!

As I have told this story over the years, the people of Brighton—especially the men—could not believe that I drove a gas tanker at such a young age. Looking at my 5'1" stature, many of them could not believe that I drove it *at any age!*

My story of driving the Gulf Limited even made it into the *Tiger Rag*, Memphis State's student newspaper. Of course, the audience that I was most concerned about was Mother. Her only comment was: "It is a good thing I didn't know about it while it was happening!"

A Sleigh Ride to Remember

One cold January morning when I was fourteen years old, I was awakened by the sound of tapping on the window. As I opened my eyes, I saw my mother standing in my room and tapping on the window pane. "Get up!" she exclaimed! "Look outside. We have *snow*!" As I jumped out of bed and pressed my nose to the glass, I saw what had made Mother so excited. Overnight, at least eight inches of snow had fallen, a rare event in Brighton, Tennessee. Mother, who had grown up on a Texas ranch southwest of San Antonio, was always more excited about the snow than even we children were.

As I stared out the window, I felt that I was in a world of white glistening glass. Everything was covered with white, fluffy snow. As the wind blew, the world seemed to be moving. The snow-covered limbs on all the trees swayed from side to side. The white-coated phone wires also danced gracefully in the wind. I was delighted and could not get enough of that beautiful scene.

Our infrequent snows signaled a special treat. Mother would send Rudy out to milk our two cows and bring in a supply of fresh cream. She would then go out into the yard and skim the top few inches off an untouched area of snow. She would use a large sugar scoop to take up some of the fresh snow from underneath the top layer and bring it into the kitchen. She added the snow to the fresh cream, then added vanilla flavoring and a generous scoop of sugar and stirred it creating a wonderful dish of "snow cream," one of the sweetest memories of my childhood.

Later that morning, about 11:00, I heard tinkling bells outside. Mother and I looked at each other and immediately realized what it was. We stepped outside in time to see Sam and Bill Melton with their horse Jobe pulling their sleigh up our street. Jobe was a large brown horse, and his name was attributed to the fact that he was frequently getting into trouble. Sam and Bill were both teenagers, just a little older than I. Their parents owned a farm out east of Brighton. When we got enough snow, they would frequently hitch Jobe to their sleigh, signaling more winter fun ahead.

Sam and Bill stopped at our house and asked Mother and me if we wanted to go for a ride. Of course we did! We eagerly agreed and went inside to bundle up. Soon we came out wearing layers and got into the sleigh. The boys put the large dark blue blanket over us and off we went. Sam took us for a quick spin up Murray hill to the sawmill and back to the house. In the meantime, Bill had gone across the street to the Hindman home to see if my friend Nell Hindman could join us. Miss Pauline, Nell's mother, felt that Nell should not go along because Nell had just recovered from being sick. Finally, Miss Pauline gave in to Nell's pleading and agreed to

allow her to go along for a "short trip." It lasted all
afternoon!

We took off from our house heading east past the Murray
house and the sawmill again and on down toward the arch
that carried the railroad track over our street. There were
two such arches in town, and this was called north arch. The
tinkling bells on the horse's harness echoed off the arch as
we passed through and out into the business area of
Brighton.

First, we passed on the right the office of Dr. Billy McLister
and his son Waldo and the drug store that they owned. On
the north side of the street was a grocery store also owned by
the McListers. Next came a barber shop that was used by the
black people in town. Then came another grocery store
owned by the Wells family, a dry goods store owned by a
Jewish merchant who was new to the community, and finally
the Baird Brothers Hardware that was managed by our
Uncle Knox. Across the street, before we came to the main
street through Brighton, we passed the Baird Brothers
General Mercantile and the Baird Brothers Ice House that
were both managed by my father, JB.

At the corner, Sam pulled on the right rein and called
"Gee," and Jobe turned right on to the main street through
town. The bells on the harness announced our passing of
still another grocery store, the Post Office, the Brighton
Savings Bank, the Robertson General Store, a small
restaurant run by Mr. Hans Anderson and his wife Violet,
and the Majestic Hotel with its wide porches, but without the
rockers that were so often used in warmer weather.

On the left side of the street were a string of private residences including the homes of my friends the DeWeese family, the McListers, and a home that was owned by the Illinois Central Railroad that they used to house whomever was the current local depot manager and his family.

At the second street, Sam pulled on the left rein and hollered "Haw," and Jobe turned left onto the street that took us past the Associate Reformed Presbyterian Church. I remember seeing more and more trees covered with snow, and I felt that I was riding through a winter wonderland. As we got to the end of the block, we turned left rather than head into the school grounds. The bandstand and other structures on the school grounds stood coated in white, but they served as reminders of warmer days when they were the center of various festivals and picnics held on these grounds every summer.

At the next street we turned left again, and a block later we had come back to the main street. Turning right, we retraced our steps for a block and then turned left again to find ourselves in front of the Baird Brothers stores. Mother asked, "Is anyone hungry?" Before we could respond, Mother directed Sam to pull up in front of the store, and she invited us all to come in for something to eat.

When we got inside, Daddy invited all of us to have some lunch. He offered everyone a sandwich and a coke, and Mother added that lunch would be free. We all huddled around the pot-belly stove trying to warm up after our ride in the cold. Many mornings when Daddy loaded up that "Warm Morning" stove with so much coal that the vent pipe from the stove to the wall turned red, Mother would warn him that some day he was going to burn down the store. Today, I was happy for all the warmth that we absorbed from that big stove.

As we were warming ourselves, Daddy went outside and unhitched Jobe, the horse, and walked him over to the Baird Brothers Livery Stables, which was behind his store and just east of the I.C. Railroad tracks. Daddy got Jobe in out of the weather and gave him some food, water, and a place to rest while we ate our lunch.

I remember watching Daddy's helper, Miss Clyde Huffman (an unusual name for a woman), prepare the sandwiches for us. I also remember sitting on the check-out counter while we ate our lunch of sandwiches, cookies, and cokes.

After lunch, we loaded up the sleigh again and took off for another ride. Mother stayed back at the store this time, so it was just us kids. This time we headed west through the north arch, up Murray Hill, past our house and all the way up to the "new" Rt. 51. We turned left onto Rt. 51, not worrying about the traffic on a day when there had been eight inches of snow. After one block, we turned left again and headed down what our family called Nelms Hill toward the south arch. I don't know what other people called it, but to us, it was Nelms Hill because the Nelms family lived there. One block past the arch, we came to the main street again where Uncle Knox lived in a big house on the corner. From this point, we continued east out of town to the Melton's farm and stopped there for a visit.

Elizabeth Melton was the mother of Sam and Bill. She had been ill; otherwise, she would have gone with us for the sleigh ride. While the boys took Jobe to his stable to rest, Mrs. Melton invited Nell and me into the parlor where a welcoming fire was burning in the fireplace. When the boys joined us, Mrs. Melton asked if we would like some popcorn. Instead of the usual covered pot like the one we used in our house, Mrs. Melton produced a square wire box with kernels inside. We waited with excitement as she held it over the fire and heated the kernels. In front of our eyes, the kernels popped into fluffy white popcorn! We actually could see it happening!

Later the boys showed us their record player. The records we played at home were flat and shaped like a plate with a hole in the middle. Our records fit over the small post in the middle of a turntable. The Meltons had an older phonograph called an "Edison." Their records were shaped like a tin can that was open on both ends. They slipped it over a circular arm and the music played. Fascinating!

We spent a wonderful afternoon eating popcorn, listening to music, and playing games. Eventually, it was time to go home. Once again, the boys harnessed the horse and took us back to town, the bells jingling all the way. We stopped at the store to let Mother and Daddy know we were on our way home. With one last handful of free candy, we went out to the sleigh and back up the hill to home. That wonderful sleigh ride has provided me with many happy memories for almost eighty years.

Just Passing Through

The Great Depression created a new set of people we called hobos. I guess they were not an entirely new thing, but there sure were more of them. As these homeless men passed through Brighton, Mother was generous when they stopped at our house. She was always willing to offer them a meal or something to eat and drink, but she clearly communicated to them her expectation that they would do something to earn that generosity. Some of them chopped wood or brought wood in from the stockpile to the house. Others would do work around the yard or the barn.

Mother noticed that many hobos would turn onto our street, pass the first house on the corner, and come directly to our back door. One day she asked one of the men about this odd phenomenon. She especially wanted to know if they had a way of marking the houses where help had been given previously so that hobos who followed them would know where they were more likely to get a handout. This fellow reluctantly admitted that they did have a sign that they used to indicate where other hobos would be likely to get help, but he would not tell Mother what the sign was. Mother and many of the neighbors gathered one day to discuss what

kind of mark they might be using, and they looked all
around our house, but they never figured it out.

I especially remember one hobo whose name was Billy Zink.
Billy was originally from Germany, and his English was not
the best. Unlike most of the hobos, Billy stayed around
Brighton for quite some time. He took his meals with our
family and slept in the house out back where our nanny and
household help, Grace Fayne, usually stayed. Billy showed
up at one of those times when Grace was off visiting her
family, so the house was temporarily available.

When he was not working around town, Billy tried to teach
us children German. He was very kind and patient in telling
us the German words for all of the items that regularly filled
our world.

In addition to the work that he did for us, he especially
earned his keep the evening he entered our house and
noticed that the exhaust pipe that led from the kitchen stove
to the chimney was red hot, indicating that there was a fire
in the flu. Billy sounded the alarm and quickly took action.
He dragged the kitchen table over under the section of the
pipe that went into the flu and put a kitchen chair on top of
the table. Mother, alerted by Billy's shouts, had already
grabbed the baking soda. She handed it to him as he
climbed up on the chair and pulled the flu pipe away from
the wall. By pouring the baking soda onto the fire, Billy was
able to extinguish it before it spread! We were all grateful for
Billy's alertness, courage, and quick action that likely saved
our house from burning.

One day Billy announced that it was time for him to move on. He thanked Mother and Daddy for all that they had done for him, and he declared that he was going to "hop a train" the next day. Sure enough, that next day, Billy was gone.

I was left with a question in my mind about how one "hops a train." The only kind of hop that I knew was the kind of short jump one did when playing "Hop Scotch," and I wondered how that would help you get on a train. Daddy patiently explained that "hopping a train" meant that a person would wait until a train was moving slowly entering or leaving a station, and would then jump onto the ladder or into an open car. I thought about that a lot, but never tried it myself.

It was true that Billy was "just passin' through," but his time with us left a lasting impression in the lives of our family.

With the Blink of an Eye: A Near-Death Experience

When a woman died in our part of the country, even in the early decades of the 20th century, it was the custom for other women in the town to prepare the body. This was prior to the current custom of professional embalming. Usually, friends of the deceased or a set of townspeople volunteered to help with this kind-but-difficult task. Mother was involved so frequently that the undertaker remarked that he always expected to see her when he was called for the death of a woman in Brighton.

In this tradition, a compassionate team of ladies was called because Mrs. Ella Smithson had died. Lela, joined by Mrs. Lilly Smith and Mrs. Bertha Hindman, showed up to help prepare her for burial. After bathing Mrs. Smithson's body, they prepared her funeral dress by cutting it up the back so they could put it on her.

As they moved her gently and worked to get her arms into the sleeves of the dress, one of the ladies shrieked, "*Wait! She's blinking her eyes!*" Alarmed, the others looked, and they saw it too!

Quickly they found a mirror and held it under her nose. The mirror steamed up with her breath! She wasn't dead after all!

Frightened yet relieved, they called the undertaker in Covington, Mr. John Eckford, who came to the house and confirmed that, indeed, Mrs. Smithson was still alive. They immediately sent for medical help.

Mrs. Smithson lived many years after that near-death experience—but, for sure, she had to buy at least one new dress.

Brighton on the Fourth of July

Dear Reader,

*Lela and JB Baird's three children—Rudolph, LaNelle, and Vivian—
lived in or near Brighton most of their lives and maintained a close
family bond. As they aged, face-to-face visits became difficult to arrange.
Vivian could no longer drive; Uncle Rudy had moved from Brighton to
an assisted living arrangement in Covington, and he had a severe hearing
loss that made communication by phone impractical. Not surprisingly,
though, Vivian did not allow such roadblocks to curtail her
communication with her brother Rudy, whom she called Buddy.*

*In her late eighties, my mother asked me to purchase a fax machine and
teach her how to use it. That was an easy request to fill so we set her
up, and she routinely faxed handwritten letters to Rudy at the assisted
living center where the staff delivered them to him. It was a terrific use
of technology that kept them in touch!*

*In going through her papers after her death, I discovered many gems,
including a handwritten letter she had faxed to Uncle Rudy on July 4,
2003. In it, she reminisced about the large annual 4th of July picnic
that was a Brighton tradition for decades.*

*We have included the handwritten letter along with a transcription. We
hope you enjoy it.*

~~~ MNMcL

Dearest Buddy,

I'm wishing you a July 4th that comes back to me as a good time in our lives.

It's very early in the morning — just a short time after sunrise. In my mind I'm sitting on the steps of our front porch watching the "Country People" ride by in their wagons and buggies. They were ready for a day of fun, greeting friends and delicious food. No one would seem to mind the heat, the dust, even the flies. It was July 4th! The wagons were loaded with people and food. Some of the wagons had one regular wagon seat and the others space held chairs, boxes, baskets and even trunks! Each box, basket, and trunk held the best food that the mother could make. For days the kitchen was the busiest place in the home. Many cakes, pies, cookies and different foods were prepared for the Big Day! Each family brought extra food just in case there were people

who would be their guests.
Beside the desserts there was alway
fried chicken. The mother would
"rescue" the "fryers" from the coop
as they were nice and fat because
they had been fed especially for
this day. Often there was a whole
ham from the smokehouse - that
had been boiled in the big iron
pot in the back yard. Jars of fried
sausage which had been fried last
winter and canned in half gallon
jars, was placed in biscuit and
made a delicious sandwich.
Of course there were 3 stands where
food could be bought. J.B. usually
had 1 or 2 of the stands
I must quit this and do some work!
Buddy, please write down some of your
memories about the picnics, reunions
anything for Me, Lynn & especially Mary Nell.
Be thinking! Love,
Sister Bill.

Dearest Buddy,

I'm wishing you a July 4th that comes back to me as a good time in our lives.

It's very early in the morning, just a short time after sunrise. In my mind I'm sitting on the steps of our front porch watching the "Country People" ride by in their wagons and buggies. They were ready for a day of fun, greeting friends and delicious food. No one would seem to mind the heat, the dust, even the flies. It was July 4th! The wagons were loaded with people and food. Some of the wagons had one regular wagon seat and the other space held chairs, boxes, baskets, and even trunks! Each box, basket, and trunk held the best food that the mother could make. For days the kitchen was the busiest place in the home. Many cakes, pies, cookies and different foods were prepared for the Big Day!

Each family brought extra food just in case there were people who would be their guests. Besides the desserts, there was always fried chicken. The mother would "rescue" the "fryers" from the coop as they were nice and fat because they had been fed especially for this day. Often there was a whole ham from the smokehouse that had been boiled in the big iron pot in the back yard. Jars of fried sausage which had been fried last winter and canned in half gallon jars was placed in biscuits and made a delicious sandwich!

Of course there were 3 stands where food could be bought. JB usually had 1 or 2 of the stands.

I must quit this and do some work. Buddy, please write down some of your memories about the picnics, reunions, anything for me, Lynn & especially Mary Nelle.

Be thinking!

Love,

Sister Bill

Part Four
Foolishness and Fun

Vivian and Rudy Baird

Thanksgiving Memories:
Bitter and Sweet

Frequently at Thanksgivings now, I think back to one particular Thanksgiving Day when I was a child. It brings memories both bitter and sweet.

Our family's custom at that time was to get all dressed up, pack up some of Mother's finest food, and go to the Salem Associate Reformed Presbyterian (ARP) Church for the church's annual Thanksgiving celebration. This was a large annual gathering of people from surrounding Presbyterian churches. For many, it was a homecoming.

While my family normally attended the Brighton ARP Church for our Thanksgiving feast, we went back to the Salem Church where Baird family members had attended in the past. Many of our Baird and McCalla ancestors on my father's side are buried in the Salem Church cemetery, and it was always a special time when we visited there.

Thanksgiving was, of course, a day of giving thanks, but also of remembering our families and of eating—plenty of eating! After a morning worship service, food that each family brought was laid out on tables that had been spread on the lawn. There was no shortage of good food, and we all enjoyed a bountiful Thanksgiving meal. After the dinner, the adults went back into the church for meetings having to do with the business of churches and the operation of the cemetery. We children were expected to stay outside for the afternoon and play "quiet" games.

On this particular Thanksgiving Day, I had on my new Lindbergh hat. It was my latest "play pretty," a term that we used for a child's favorite toy. Earlier, Charles Lindbergh had crossed the Atlantic in the world's first non-stop, transatlantic solo flight. This landmark event not only captured the fascination and imagination of almost everybody around the globe, but it also caught the attention of all sorts of marketers, manufacturers, and opportunists. This led to a huge variety of souvenirs that capitalized on the Lindbergh name and his famous achievement. My memento was a genuine Lindbergh hat!

My special hat was a felt beanie that had a separate felt border around the lower part of the crown. Attached to this border was another piece of fabric that was turned up and was embroidered with images of planes, each a different color. On the front of the cap was the part that I really loved —the propeller! This wooden propeller was two inches long, and it was mounted on a stack of small squares of felt to lift it above the rest of the hat. When I ran, the propeller would spin. The faster I ran, the faster it whirled!

As we children played our "quiet" games in the churchyard, one of the older girls grabbed my special hat off my head and ran away. When I ran after her to get my hat back, she threw it to another child, and the game was on. The more I chased it from child to child, the more upset I got and the more fun the other children had. When someone pitched to a boy named Calvin, he noticed that it had a loose thread. Naturally, he had to see what would happen if he pulled that thread. And, of course, as he tugged at it, more thread came undone, and the hat began to come apart. Someone tossed it back to the older girl who started it all, and she gave the thread one last yank. My cherished hat fell apart! She tossed the remains to Minnie, who was my good friend. Minnie ended the game by giving me the hat—or what was left of it.

I was one unhappy little soul. I was sadly looking at the parts of my ruined hat just as the adults began coming out of church. I took the parts of my hat to Mother and told her what had happened. With great sympathy, Mother assured me that the hat was very simply made and could easily be repaired. She would take care of it when we got home.

As the grown ups came outside, Daddy noticed that a dark cloud was forming. Everyone quickly began to leave for their homes. Getting home to Brighton that day was no easy matter, however. As we drove away from the church and got a few miles up Portersville Road the rain came down in torrents.

The Model T Ford did not have windows that could be rolled up to keep out the rain and wind. What it did have were leather-like curtains that had isinglass windows in them. Isinglass looked like what we would today regard as light plastic. The curtains were flexible, but they were effective in keeping out the rain. They were stored under the back seat of the T Model, as it was casually called. They had to be stretched over the window openings then attached to the car's frame. The curtains had a series of eyelets around the edges, and the window frames had a series of posts that matched up with the eyelets. Each eyelet was placed over a post, then a movable section of the post was turned down to hold the curtain in place. It was a time-consuming process that would be very unpleasant to do in the rain.

Just as the rain increased to the point where the curtains were necessary, Daddy noticed that the gate in the fence of Bob Strong's property was standing open, as was the door to his barn. Without hesitating, Daddy quickly turned onto the Strong's property and drove right into the hall down the middle of their barn! This took us out of the rain, and we could take our time attaching the curtains!

The shelter of the barn also gave Daddy an opportunity to attach chains to the wheels. Because the dirt roads around Brighton got very soft and muddy during rainstorms, we sometimes needed chains on the wheels to get enough traction to go up hills. When faced with steep hills on a muddy road, Daddy would turn the car around and go up the hill in reverse because that also improved the traction.

After attaching the curtains and the chains, we were back on our way. The steepest hill came just before we reached Brighton. After backing up that hill and turning around to go forward again, we could see the Brighton Depot not too far in the distance. We were thankful to see it because that meant that we would soon be home.

When we were safely back home, we remembered that it was Thanksgiving Day, and we were grateful for the safe return. And I was especially grateful that Mother was going to fix my Lindbergh hat!

See-Sawing Through the Fence

It was 1910 when Mother and Daddy first moved into their new house on a hill in Brighton. That was seven years before I was born, and the property lines with the adjoining neighbors were open and uncluttered. There was a wonderful open feeling to it and a nice view that mother loved. Perhaps it reminded her of the wide open spaces of the Texas ranch south of San Antonio where she grew up. But, at some point in time, a six-foot high wooden fence was built between the side yard of the Baird house and the yard of our neighbor to the west. I am not sure who built and owned that fence, but I am certain that Mother despised it.

At first, Mother tried to hide the fence by planting flowers along it. She put tall red cannas immediately beside the fence and lower blooming plants in front of the cannas. In spite of this beautiful curtain of flowers, the fence was still visible and hardly a day passed when Mother did not say how much she hated it.

Finally, Mother adopted the philosophy that "if you can't beat 'em, join 'em." She could not make the fence disappear, so she decided to find a use for it. One day she came across a large wooden plank out back by the barn, and that gave her an idea. She contacted a "jackleg" carpenter in town and hired him to cut a hole in the fence. (*"Jackleg" was an expression for a semi-trained, self-made member of a trade who was not considered a full-fledged tradesman.*) The opening he cut was about three feet off the ground and was large enough to easily accommodate the plank Mother had found. Once the hole was cut, Mother slid the plank halfway through it, and, presto! We had a see-saw!

The kids from all over the neighborhood gathered in the yard, and Mother gave us all a lesson in the fine points of see-sawing. Children straddled the plank on both sides of the fence and used their collective weight to push their end of the plank toward the ground, giving their friends on the other side of the fence a lift toward the sky. Usually the two groups cooperated in giving each other fun rides up and down while little hands held tightly to the plank.

I remember that when our side was down, we could see the faces of our friends high up in the air above the fence. When they pushed down, we had our chance to look over the fence and see them crouched near the ground. Sometimes the low end of the plank hit the ground so hard that the kids on the up end almost bounced off! I remember being frightened that we might be bounced off the plank when we were up in the air and go crashing to the ground below.

Most of the time, the cooperative play that provided all of us the rhythmic opportunities to be up then down, up then down, did not last too long. It was too hard for the kids on the end that had the most weight to resist trapping the other kids in the air. The kids who were being held above the fence would holler to be let down, and the blackmailers on the other side of the fence would extract wild promises from them. Shortly, their promises changed to threats that Mother would be "told" if they weren't let down. The alliances were constantly changing, and the youngest children would try to get the bigger kids on their side so they would be able to maroon my older brother Rudy in the air against his will.

The see-saw sessions didn't last a long time each time we did it, but we used that plank often, and we always obeyed the one rule of see-sawing at the Baird home—after we finished, the children were responsible for passing the plank through the cut to the Baird side of the fence and laying it down flat and out of the way alongside the driveway. There it would stay until the next time the children transformed the ugly fence into a fun toy.

A Ride to Rialto

Every summer of my childhood, as far back as I can remember, my friends Eunice and Louise Billings came to visit their grandparents for a vacation. It was my good fortune that their grandparents, Mr. and Mrs. Will Billings, lived across the street from us, so I had two extra friends in the neighborhood for much of the summer. Eunice was the same age as I, and Louise was about two years older. We had great fun, and we were always sorry to see their vacation end.

One year, as they were getting ready to go home, they asked, "Can you come to see us sometime?" Eunice and Louise lived in Rialto, Tennessee, a small town about fifteen miles north of Brighton. Mother said, "Maybe we could do that some day. Let me think about it."

Little did I know that Mother was probably already spinning another adventure for me. Rialto was on the north-south line of the Illinois Central Railroad that ran through Brighton, and she must have felt that, at age eight, I was ready for my first solo train trip. Later that summer, she arranged for me to take the train to Rialto and spend a couple nights with Eunice and Louise.

I had no fear of riding the train. Once before, when I was three years old, we had taken the train all the way to Texas. I felt like an old pro, even though that trip to San Antonio included a wreck of the train we were on, so we had to change to a different one for the rest of the journey. I'm not sure how much of that experience I really remember, or how much I remembered hearing the rest of the family talk about the wreck, although I do remember being scared when it happened. But now, at eight, I felt like a really big girl!

In preparation for this great adventure, mother made me a new nightgown. She sewed it using soft pink fabric that she brought home from the store. She also made it with straps! "*Straps! Wow!*" I'd always had little girl gowns and had never had a nightgown with straps! And to complete the surprise, she embroidered this beautiful pink gown with different colored flowers across the front and on each strap. I felt like I'd arrived before I had even departed! A train trip *and* a nightgown with straps! I really felt grown up!

When the day for my trip arrived, I was extremely excited. Mother had packed my small black suitcase with my shirts, overalls, and my new night gown, so we were ready to go. As we walked to the car, my dog "Spooks," a white terrier with brown spots, ran ahead of us and jumped into the car as if he were going, too. Before heading to the depot, we stopped at Daddy's store so I could tell him good-bye.

He said, "Now while you're gone, remember your manners."
"Yes, Daddy," I replied, smiling like the big brave girl he
encouraged me to be.

It was only a five-minute ride to the railroad depot at the
south end of town. We arrived early and were greeted by
Mr. Tommy Goulder, the station officer. While we waited, he
was tapping out a noisy message. I asked Mother, "What is
that 'click-click' machine?" She promptly repeated my
question to Mr. Goulder, and they both took great delight in
my renaming of his Morse Code transmitter. He invited me
behind the counter to see how he was sending the message.
Before my train arrived, we were lucky enough to witness a
telegraph message come into the office. Mr. Goulder
interpreted it to me as he listened to it. To this day, I don't
understand how he was able to make sense out of all those
fast clicks!

Soon we heard the howling whistle of the train as it
approached the Brighton Station. Carrying my suitcase in
one hand and holding onto Mother with the other, I walked
out to the tracks with her. Mr. Goulder went ahead of us
carrying a large wooden stool. When the train came to a full
stop, we stood back until several passengers got off the train
by first stepping down onto the wooden stool Mr. Goulder
had placed at the door. When the way was clear, Mr.
Goulder invited us to go on board, and Mother went on with
me to help me find a seat.

Mother and I walked down the aisle and selected my seat.
After she saw that I was comfortable and still excited about
the trip, she said her good-bye, gave me a big Baird hug, got

off the train, and stood next to the train near my window. Now, I was *really* feeling like a big girl!

The train started to move slowly, and I looked out and saw Mother waving her little white handkerchief. I reached into my purse and took out my own hanky and waved back at her. A lump was growing in my throat as I told myself, "*You are a big girl. You are a really big girl….*"

Before we had pulled away from the Brighton Station, the conductor approached, introduced himself, and told me not to be afraid. He said, "Part of my job is to take care of little travelers like you. That's what they pay me for." He assured me that he would make certain that I did not miss my stop in Rialto. Then I thought: "Oh, Rialto! That's right! I'm going to Rialto!" The lump disappeared, and I was excited again.

As we made our way through Covington and on toward Rialto, the conductor came and talked to me some more. I remember that we talked about our friends and family. He asked about the friends I would be visiting, and he asked about who would be meeting me at the station. Before long, I could feel the train slowing down as we pulled into Rialto. The conductor came around once again. He looked out and saw that it was raining, and he asked if I had a coat. I did not. It had been sunny in Brighton.

As the train came to a stop at the Rialto Station, it was raining very hard. I was worried till I looked out the window and saw Mr. Billings carrying a coat and a hat for me. And he held the biggest umbrella I had ever seen in my life! He met me at the door and gave me a big hug. Then he wrapped the coat around me, put the hat on my head, and carried me away.

Next came the biggest surprise of the trip—the Billings family did not own a car! He had come to pick me up in his farm wagon pulled by two mules! He carried me to the wagon, placed me down on the cold, wet, rough bench beside where he would be sitting, opened the umbrella for me, and told me, "Hold on!" Mr. Billings went around to the other side, got up onto the bench, took the leather leads, tapped each mule with his reins, and off we went on the wettest ride of my life, so far.

We arrived at the Billings home in a short time, and I was welcomed by Mrs. Billings and the squealing Eunice and Louise. We laughed about the wagon ride in the rain, and I told them about my exciting train ride. It wasn't long before Mrs. Billing called us to supper.

We gathered for supper at a very long table. Books were stacked at one end of the table, and the family sat at the other. Mrs. Billings served chicken and "dumplins." The dumplings were positively the best I had ever tasted, but Mrs. Billings did not know that I had an aversion to chicken. More about *that* later.

After supper, Eunice, Louise, and I played Old Maid and told stories. Before long, it was time for bed. As we prepared for sleep, I was proud to show off my new nightgown with its garden of flowers growing up over the straps. *I had straps!!* As we settled down, I remember feeling a pang of what must have been homesickness. This was the first night I'd ever spent away from all the members of my family, but I was sharing a huge bed with Eunice and Louise and the fun of that took my mind away from what I was missing.

As I was drifting off, I realized that the Billings had a very heavy kind of wallpaper with designs on it. I was fascinated by the fact that it was not attached to the wall with paste. Instead, it was attached with tacks around the edges and down the seams. I remember wondering if they had bought this paper at Daddy's store. Soon I was fast asleep.

Morning came bright and sunny. That afternoon we played in the yard, which was filled with many blocks of freshly chopped wood. We played tag, jumping from block to block and trying to make the blocks rock from side to side. We were having great fun until Mrs. Billings, afraid someone might get hurt, came out and told us to stay off the blocks of wood.

I was surprised to find out that the Billings separated their wood into two types: one type for the cooking stove and another for the fireplace. I had thought that all wood was the same. It all looked alike to me. At our house, we used the same wood for both purposes. I learned that the difference in the Billings' wood pile was in how the wood was cut. Some had to be cut in smaller lengths to fit into their cooking stove.

We spent some of our time that afternoon helping Mr. Billings tidy up the yard by organizing the blocks of wood. I learned that the wood came from a tree that had been felled by lightning. Mr. Billings had cut the wood for burning, but he was not sure that it would burn properly. Some folks thought that wood from a tree struck by lightning would not burn well. I have often wondered if that's a tale or fact.

I spent two nights with the Billings family and had a lot of fun. Mother and Daddy drove to Rialto to pick me up, and when they arrived in the Model T Ford, I was very happy to see them. Daddy, knowing that the Billings did not have a car of their own, offered to take them all for a ride. We went on a brief jaunt down the road and back, and then we were ready to head for home.

On the ride back, we drove first to Covington and stopped for a visit at Grandmother Baird's place. I was the center of attention as I told about my thrilling solo train ride to Rialto. Once my time in the spotlight had passed, Grandmother sent my cousin Felix Tanner and me to the store on an errand before dinner. Once there, Felix handed the list of needed items to the clerk, and we looked around the store while waiting for our order to be filled. I was tempted by the display of candy bars and found enough money in my purse for two of them. Felix and I ate them while we waited, much to the chagrin of Mother when she found out later. As we looked around the store, I wondered why there were Christmas angels still hanging from the ceiling; Christmas had been months earlier!

Felix and I played out in the yard until suppertime. After we ate, Mother, Daddy, and I headed back to Brighton. I was anxious to get home and play with my dog Spooks. He came out and jumped on the running board of the car as we pulled into the driveway. He seemed as happy to see me as I was him.

The trip to visit my friends was very special, but there really is no place like home.

Post Note about my aversion to eating chicken:

I think the aversion to eating chicken I mentioned earlier in this story started when I watched Mother kill and prepare chickens. She killed and dressed the bird, although it always seemed to me that it should have been called "undressing" the bird since she removed all its feathers. Then, Mother poured boiling water over the chicken. This had two effects: first, it made the chicken's skin appear to be "crawling," and I always liked watching that. Second, it caused the bird to emit the most putrid, foul-smelling odor I have ever experienced. The smell was awful, but I put up with it so that I could watch that chicken's skin crawl. For years, I could not eat a piece of chicken!

Young Vivian's Driving Adventure

In 1926, my mother and father loaded my brother Rudy, my sister Nelle, and me into our Ford Model T Touring car for a three day road trip from Brighton, Tennessee, to San Antonio, Texas. Although we had made this lengthy trip several times by train to visit Mother's family, this was our first journey by car.

Our Texas family included two young cousins—nine-year old Clifton, who was the same age as I, and eleven-year old Julia. On our first day there, Clifton gave me a ride on the handlebars of his bicycle and eagerly showed me how he could keep up with the shadows of the clouds as they passed quickly along the street. This sense of competition made its way into our daily play. When visiting a friend there who owned a brand new Packard with a jump seat for two, Clifton, Julia, and I would race to see which two of us would get to ride in the jump seat.

Perhaps it was this friendly rivalry that led to my greatest adventure as a nine-year old. One afternoon, as the three of us were playing in our parked Model T, Clifton sat at the wheel pretending to drive while Julia and I perched in the back seat "being chauffeured." Casually, I announced to my cousins that I knew how to drive. They were sure I was making this up. We argued back and forth.

"Can not!"

"Can too!"

They did not realize that back home in Tennessee, my mother had allowed me to sit on her lap and steer our car as she drove along the country roads. Eventually I had learned to work the hand-operated throttle and had grown tall enough to reach and operate the three floor pedals, which were the brake, forward gears, and reverse.

To prove myself to my unbelieving cousins, I confidently made Clifton move, replaced him behind the steering wheel, and promptly started the car. Fortunately, this was the first Model T we owned that had a starter inside and did not require hand-cranking from the front grill to start the engine.

Before my shocked cousins knew what happened, we three smoothly drove off down the block heading west into local traffic! At the first corner, I turned left, continuing my impromptu drive around the block.

Before we reached the end of the block and approached the next turn, I caught a glimpse of my seventeen-year-old brother Rudy running across the neighbors' properties and on a line to head us off at the next corner. He had seen me drive off with Julia and Clifton as passengers and realized that I might need help. When he caught up with us, he jumped on the running board next to me in the driver's seat and just rode there.

Rather than having me pull over so he could take control of the car, Rudy stayed on the running board beside me and made sure that I knew what I was doing. After three more turns, we arrived back in front of our cousins' house, and I had safely completed my first solo driving adventure. I don't remember what my cousins had to say about it, but I do remember Mother lecturing me on the need to wait until I was sixteen before I drove again.

After a week or so, our father returned to Memphis by train. Three weeks later, Mother, Rudy, Nelle, and I packed up the Model T for our return. We made quite a sight, our brave, adventurous mother; three kids; a newly-acquired German shepherd puppy; and a sack of fresh onions secured neatly on the running board!

We camped our way home to Brighton—but that's another story...

Sunday Croquet—or Not?

I well remember when Daddy ordered us a new croquet set through one of the wholesale catalogs used by the Baird Brothers Hardware Store. We set it up in the front yard, and the kids in the neighborhood, seeing the colorful mallets and balls, frequently stopped by for a game. We used it often and enjoyed it a lot.

One Sunday, our family returned from Sunday School and sat down for our usual Sunday dinner. After we'd eaten this large midday meal that was a weekly tradition, some of us young ones thought it would be a good time for a few games of croquet. As we were organizing the teams, Daddy caught wind of what we were doing and called it to Mother's attention. Like a good Presbyterian, he asked, "Lela, do you know what these children are planning to do on Sunday?"

Lela responded, "No, JB. What are they planning?"

"They are planning to play croquet!" he explained, obviously distressed.

"That's nice," Lela replied calmly.

"Nice? What do you mean nice?" Daddy sputtered incredulously.

"Croquet is a nice friendly game, JB, and the children really enjoy it." Mother remained calm, successfully hiding her agitation.

"But it's the Sabbath!" he blustered.

"So?" Mother asked, her agitation beginning to show.

"We can't have the children playing croquet in the front yard on Sunday!" Daddy pronounced, being true to his Associate Reformed Presbyterian upbringing.

"Why not, JB?" Mother asked, her agitation now in full bloom.

"Why, the neighbors will see them, and what would they think!" he declared. "It's Sunday—a day of worship and rest. They are not supposed to be playing croquet on Sunday!"

"Hmmmm," Lela mused a moment. Then, with her characteristic caginess, she offered, "What if they move the game to the back yard? The neighbors won't see them there."

"Well…I guess that would be all right this once," he muttered, walking away with his value system stretched a bit.

So, with Mother's wily help, we children finally played croquet that Sunday, but not where the neighbors would see!

My Back Porch Hair Cut

In the 1920s, really daring women were having their hair "bobbed," which was a term for getting a short hair cut. This was a serious break from the age-old tradition of women having very long hair, and it really raised eyebrows back then. Many people, especially men, considered a woman's hair to be her "crowning glory" and to cut it was scandalous. "Proper" women kept their hair long, despite the bother of taking care of it.

The change to a short hair style frequently met resistance and sometimes even retaliation. When I was teaching in Burlison in 1939, I met a man who had one of the longest beards that I had ever seen. He told me that he had started growing his beard in protest when his wife first had her hair cut short; he had let his beard grow ever since. I also remember visiting one of Mother's friends whose son was an attorney. He told us about a divorce case that he was handling in which the husband had initiated divorce proceedings because his wife had her hair cut short! In those days, a woman with short hair really disturbed a lot of men, which may have been why so many women wanted to have their hair bobbed in the first place!

My mother, Lela, was one of the first women in Brighton to step forward and have short hair. She and Grace McLister had gone to Memphis and returned with a new look that was becoming all the rage for women throughout the country! This was really quite controversial, but I loved the style she wore.

As I grew up, I naturally wanted to be just like my mother. My friends Elizabeth, Helen, and Mary Ellen all had short hair. My sister Nelle, seven years older than I, had short hair. I, too, wanted my hair bobbed instead of the long curls I had always worn.

In the 1920s, the most popular style of short "bobbed" hair was the "shingled" look, a style in which the hair was cut very short at the neckline—*scandalous*! The rest of the hair was cut in soft tapers from the crown to the neck giving a soft, sloping effect.

LaNelle Baird

Even as a child, I felt it was time for me to have the shingled look, too. I was persistent in asking Mother and Daddy for permission to have my hair bobbed. They were equally persistent in telling me that I was too young for such a thing and that my long dark hair was lovely.

One Sunday morning after Sunday school, Mother gave Nelle and me permission to go home early instead of staying for the worship service. I cannot remember what excuse we used when we asked Mother to allow us to walk home early, but whatever it was, it worked. Nelle and I walked the six blocks from the church to home by ourselves.

About an hour later, Mother, Daddy, and Rudy came home from church driving our T Model. They parked the car out near the garage and came up the steps to the back porch. Right away, Mother spotted the scissors and clumps of long black hair on the back porch. I had convinced Nelle to do what Mother and Daddy had prohibited...she had "bobbed" my hair!

I proudly showed them my "shingled" look, but Mother's reaction was not what Nelle and I had hoped. I can still hear Mother's voice in her most unhappy tone:"*Who cut your hair?*" She was not only unhappy that Nelle had cut off my beautiful black locks, but she was not at all complimentary about my sister's skills as a barber.

That afternoon, Mother called on Venie Philips, a neighbor and a self-taught barber, to try to improve Nelle's handiwork. She was able to help a little, but the next day, one of Brighton's barbers, Mr. Frank Hurt, shaped up my "shingled" look even more. Some weeks later after my hair had grown in a little, Mother took me back to Mr. Hurt for a professional "shingled" hair cut.

We never again got permission to come home early from Sunday school—in fact, we never asked again!

A Watch in the Apple Orchard

In 1931, when I was fourteen years-old, my twenty-three-year-old brother Rudy was working for Tipton County as the gravel inspector. Most of the roads in the county were dirt roads at that time, but many were in the process of being "graveled." This was the term we used for spreading loose gravel on roads to make them more passable, especially in wet weather. Rudy would work at the gravel pit each day, checking the quality of the gravel that was being hauled out to the roads of Tipton County.

The gravel pit was located on Mr. Leno Mill's farm in Holly Grove, a community west of Brighton. The site was a very interesting place with a dragline right in the center of the deep pit. The dragline was a huge steam shovel, a giant to us, and it was a wonder to watch. The large arm of the shovel had a huge bucket on its end. As the dragline operated, its arm would swing up and out to lower the bucket into the earth that was rich in gravel. The machine would scoop up a huge load of small rocks and lift the bucket filled with heavy gravel, swing it out to the side, then empty its contents into the bed of one of the waiting gravel trucks. After each truck was filled, it would drive off to the area of the county where a road was being graveled. There it would dump its load, and workers would spread it on the road. In the meantime, back at the gravel pit, another truck would be waiting; the dragline would fill it and it would drive off to its destination. This routine was repeated many times each day as truck after truck returned to the pit for gravel to take out to the county's roads.

Rudy Baird, seated on a truck at the gravel pit, 1931.

At the time that Rudy was working at the gravel pit, he owned a brand new 1930 Model A Ford Coupe with a rumble seat. After my first independent driving adventure, which happened in San Antonio at age nine, I had promised Mother that I would not drive again until I reached the legal driving age of sixteen. *But…* Mother and Daddy were away on vacation for several weeks, and this was too good an opportunity to pass up…So, like the good "Buddy" he was, Rudy agreed to allow me to ride with him to the gravel pit each morning, drop him off, use his car all day while he was working, then drive back and pick him up in the late afternoon. Now remember—*I was only fourteen!*

We did this each day while our parents were away, and one afternoon, my friend Nell Hindman rode with me to pick up

Rudy. We arrived a bit early and looked around for something to do. Then we spied Mr. Mills' apple orchard near by. As we waited for Rudy, we stealthily helped ourselves to three apples—one each for Rudy, Nell, and me. I was sure that Mr. Mills would not mind!

At home that evening, I realized that my pretty wristwatch was not on my arm! I searched all around the house and in Rudy's Model A for several days, but there was no sign of it anywhere. It was truly missing.

A few days later, Mr. Mills was talking to Rudy and casually asked him, "Do you know anyone who has lost a wristwatch?" He showed Rudy the watch, and Rudy recognized it immediately.

"That's my sister's watch!" answered Rudy innocently. "She must have lost it one day she came to pick me up after work."

Then he asked Mr. Mills where he found it.

"In my apple orchard!" Mr. Mills responded forcefully!

Rudy put it all together and offered to pay Mr. Mills for the three apples we had enjoyed. Mr. Mills did not accept the payment offer, but he sure got his fun by teasing me that I was going to jail! I always felt grateful to Mr. Mills for the three juicy apples and no jail time!

Roller Skating in Brighton

They say that travel broadens your knowledge about the world, and our family's brief stay at a friend's house in Texas did that for me. On a trip to visit my mothers's family in San Antonio, we stayed two nights in Dallas with one of Mother's friends, Belle Bolick. Belle had lived in Brighton for many years, but had moved to Texas a few years earlier.

The Bolicks had a beautiful new house, and my sister Nelle and I stayed in a large bedroom that had twin beds. In between the beds was a table that held a beautiful glass lamp with roses etched in the glass base. What was most interesting to us was that the lamp was "electric." Our lamps at home were Aladdin lamps that burned kerosene. They required us to strike a match and use it to light the lamp's wick. To light the electric lamp, we only had to flip a switch! And we did! Repeatedly! Nelle and I were fascinated by the instant light that did not require a match. For us, it was *matchless!*

The next day, I looked outside to see the neighborhood children skating on the sidewalk. While I had seen roller skates before, I had never had an opportunity to try them. I made friends with the children, and they helped me strap the skates to my shoes and tighten them with a key. The kids helped me stand up, and they pulled me along the sidewalk. When they turned me loose, I could walk on the skates, but I was too frightened to try skating on my own. Despite that, I was hooked! Once we got home to Brighton, Mother bought me my own set of roller skates, and I set about teaching myself how to skate.

First, I started skating in the house where there were walls to hang on to and keep me from falling. When I got comfortable enough, I moved to the sidewalk and learned to skate without the walls. As I was developing this skill, Mother reminded me that one of the first plates that I ate from as a very small child had a picture of a little girl on roller skates. As I was learning to talk, I would tell Mother that "I going to "kool on roller kates." In spite of my poor articulation, they knew what I meant. As I got to be a better skater, I eventually fulfilled that early promise, and I did, in fact, 'kate to 'kool many days.

As I began skating on the sidewalks through the town of Brighton, I remember Mr. Walter Ash, one of the town's peace officers, telling me that I should not be skating on the sidewalks. That scared me, and I went to the store to tell Daddy what had happened. Daddy calmly went to talk to Mr. Ash.

Daddy asked him, "Did she run into someone? Had she bothered somebody?"

Mr. Ash said, "No, but the sidewalks are not made for skating."

Daddy replied that I had as much right to be on the sidewalk as anyone else. Then he came back to me and told me, "Go ahead and skate, just be careful not to bump into anyone. If someone is coming toward you on the sidewalk, stop and step off to the side until they pass. Go ahead and skate, but just be careful."

I heeded Daddy's caution and went on to skate through Brighton more and more. I even skated on the new Highway 51! I learned to use one of Mother's brooms to control my speed when zooming down the steep hill on Rt. 51. When I got to the bottom of the hill, I would toss the broom to the side of the road and pick it up on my way home. Of course, it was much slower going back up that big hill!

My friends Helen and Kathryne DeWese had an uncle that we all loved. He introduced himself as "Lenox Leno Peter Jumbo Morrison." The nieces called him Uncle Leno, but to the Baird children, he was Mr. Leno. He was quite a character, and he always created a lot of fun.

Mr. Leno loved to skate and was really good at it. He would frequently join me for some roller skating around Brighton. We would often skate on short stretches of the newly paved Rt. 51, which was first opened in 1926. It was smooth and perfect for skating.

On my sixteenth birthday, Mr. Leno and I took off on a special adventure to roller skate all the way from Brighton to

Covington on Highway 51! There was not much traffic on the road at that time, so it was fairly safe. We stopped to rest and talk several times along the way, so it took us a few hours to make the trip. Miss Mildred, Mr. Leno's wife, drove to Covington and met us at the Union Drug Store where we all enjoyed ice cream cones to celebrate my birthday and the success of our adventure. After our celebration, Mr. Leno and I gladly accepted Miss Mildred's offer to give us a ride back up the hill to Brighton!

The Baird Barn Theater

Barns were the original multi-purpose centers of rural communities in America. They were the center of farming life, providing shelter for the animals and storage for their feed. They also served as indoor gathering spaces for parties and square dances. In the movies, they were used often for trysts by young lovers and for refuge by fugitives on the lam. For us, they were a great place to play and to stage our original plays.

The Baird barn was built in 1910 and had two levels. The animal stalls and the corn crib were located on the bottom level, and the hay was stored on the second level in the hay loft. On the east side of the first level, there were three stalls and then the corn crib where corn and sweet-smelling cow feed were stored. The crib had a higher ceiling than the stalls, and this resulted in a three-foot rise that created a tall platform up in the hay loft, on the east side of the barn. This platform was perfect as a stage, and the rest of the space, emptied of hay for the summer, was ready-made for an audience.

During the summer between my fifth and sixth grades, the other children in the neighborhood and I decided to put on a play. Almost all of the kids were involved, the DeWese girls, the Hurts, the Smiths, the Johnsons, the Hindmans, and the Bairds. Like kids of all ages, we wanted to "perform" for our parents. While there was no television to influence us, we all had been entertained every summer by the Chautauqua so we knew about stage plays.

The very word "Chautauqua" conjures up many fun and entertaining memories. The Chautauqua was a company from New York that made a circuit of many small towns and came to Brighton every summer when I was a child. People would gather in the large study hall of Brighton School every evening for a week to hear lectures on a variety of topics such as religion, philosophy, and politics, and to enjoy classic plays, musicals, bell ringers, and all sorts of entertainment, including the first moving picture shows that we ever saw. Those were called silent movies because they had no dialogue, but there were plenty of musical accompaniments. I can still remember the hum of the projector as we watched our first-ever movies!

For our theater in the barn, the older girls wrote our first play, but all of us got involved in creating our theater and in the acting. You cannot have a play without a curtain to pull, so first we needed a curtain. Mother donated a couple of bed sheets for us to decorate. When I went to Daddy at the store to ask for paint for the "curtain," he declined. There was plenty of paint, but Daddy did not want us using it on his front porch. Instead, he gave us two large boxes of crayons.

We gathered other supplies from our houses and from the barn, and the work began. Mother suggested that we spread the sheets on the east side of the store's front porch where they would be out of the way of people coming and going through the front door. We then had to decide on what to create. All ideas were welcome, but not all were workable. We eventually decided on a scene. The coloring of the sheets was done by Kathryne, Alene, and Helen DeWese and by my sister Nelle and me. It took us days. We rolled the sheets up every night so the dogs would not get on them. I do not recall who came up with the idea, but we created a curtain that a had a blue sky with a big yellow sun, tall green trees, and red and yellow flowers all over the ground. One of the big debates was whether the sun was coming up or going down. Because the stage ran from east to west and the sun was on the right side as the audience faced it, I guess we decided that the sun was going down.

My brother Rudy and his friend Gerald Hindman also helped out. They were older than the rest of us, but they added their construction talents. They collected old planks and used them to make benches. They scraped and cleaned them and made them ready for the audience. They found a pipe in the barn's downstairs hall that was a perfect length to cross the width of the upstairs stage. They threaded a wire through it so they could hang it. Then the pipe and its wire were threaded through the hem on the top of the curtain. We all watched with excitement as Rudy and Gerald raised the pipe and the curtain. Next they attached them to the west wall on one side of the stage and to a conveniently located upright on the east side. Even if we were to never stage a play, we were thrilled by the sight of our hand-painted curtain!

While I do not recall any of the plays that we performed, most of my memories center on the curtain. Two very important members of the cast were the "curtain pullers." These jobs were ably filled by Jack Hindman and Felix Tanner. When the guests arrived, the curtain was closed. At show time, one of the "curtain pullers," usually Jack, would step out from behind the curtain, welcome the audience, and thank them for coming. Then he would step back behind the curtain, and he and Felix would open the curtain by each walking one half of it to his side of the stage. When the play ended, the curtain pullers would close the curtain. Then, the one who did not do the welcoming would step out and give the farewell. He would once again, thank the audience for coming.

For our audience, coming to the play was no easy matter. Because our theater was on the second floor of the barn, our guests had to climb a ladder to get to the show. The ladder did not stand out away from the wall at an angle, but consisted of individual rungs that were nailed to the wall of the barn. There was barely enough room between the rungs and the wall for the front part of a foot to land, and most of our attendees were women who were not accustomed to making such an awkward climb, especially in their long dresses. There was a lot of teasing among them about climbing the ladder! I'm not sure that very many of us as spry youngsters at the time appreciated what a sacrifice this was for our mothers and neighbors to make the climb up the ladder to the Baird Barn Theater.

Following the show and the drama of our guests getting down from the hay loft, the cast was available for autographs on the front porch. Mother always served iced tea and fresh-baked cookies.

The Baird Barn Theater was used for several summers. Even after the plays ended, the curtain hung there for many years as evidence of our creativity, the influence of the Chautauqua, and the kind indulgence of our parents.

Mama Lela's Near-Miss

When my brother Rudy was a young man, he had a friend whose name was Maurice Coats. Maurice owned a very popular restaurant in Covington called the U-Cum-Inn. This was the first restaurant that I remembered where you ordered the food from your car and your order was brought out by one of a very effective group of carhops. These carhops knew all the customers by name, and they made your visit a lot of fun.

The U-Cum-Inn was most popular with the young people of the area who flocked to the restaurant after ball games and school dances. There was a lower parking lot behind the Inn where many of the kids would gather. Restaurant staff would keep an eye on things and make sure that there was no funny business going on out there.

One of Maurice's hobbies was flying. Airplanes were still quite a novelty when I was in high school in the early 1930s, so knowing someone who flew his own airplane was very unusual. Because my brother Rudy was a close friend of Maurice, he had many opportunities to fly with him.

Frequently, we would hear Maurice's plane circling over Brighton, and we would look up and wave to him and Rudy.

Other members of our family also had an opportunity to go flying with Maurice. I remember taking off from the Covington airport and flying north over Ripley and all the way to Dyersburg. Then we circled and flew south toward Memphis. Before landing, we flew over Brighton, but I was not able to make out very much on the ground. I do remember repaying Maurice for this adventure by making him a box of homemade candy, which my brother Rudy delivered for me.

Mother, in her typical readiness for adventure, was also excited about getting a chance to fly with Maurice. One day her turn came, and she really enjoyed her thrilling tour over the west Tennessee countryside. The very next day following Mother's flight with Maurice, he took off from the Covington airport and suddenly noticed that the engine did not sound right. Before he could do anything about it, the entire engine completely fell off the plane and landed in the garden of some unsuspecting neighbor!

Maurice was able to successfully glide the plane back to a safe landing in a near-by field, and, for a long time, Mother had great fun recounting how close she came to being in a plane crash.

A Surprise Drop-In

During the summer of my ninetieth year, I was spending a pleasant late afternoon in my "outdoor parlor" with my former student, Glenn, who did a lot of yard work for me. My outdoor parlor was a grouping of vintage metal lawn chairs under the large oak tree in front of my house on McLennan Road. We were having a pleasant conversation with a neighbor and her sons when Glenn commented on a helicopter that was flying overhead.

The helicopter grew closer, then seemed to be circling my property. Our place isn't in a usual flight pattern so such sightings are infrequent in our part of Tipton County. I became a little concerned because helicopters have circled over our neighborhood when law enforcement was searching for escapees from the detention facility near Mason, about fifteen miles east of my house and farm in Clopton.

As the helicopter circled again, our concern grew. Soon it began to descend, getting lower and lower. My farm seemed to be its focus!

I held my breath, then we were all shocked when the chopper landed in the open field just west of our house and driveway! My vision was dim due to Macular Degeneration so Glenn alerted me, saying: "Miss Vivian! The pilot's getting out!"

Sure enough, the roar of the motor died down, the rotor on the helicopter stopped spinning, and the side door opened. A distinguished-looking gentleman got out and began walking toward us! I could not help but wonder what new problem I was about to face.

As I got up off of my chair, I heard the pilot call out, *"Hey, Miss Vivian! It's me, Mike Hopkins!"*

What a surprise—and relief! I had frequently said to Mike, "Why don't you drop in some time?" I guess he took me literally!

Mike had been one of my students when he was in the sixth grade. After graduating, he got involved with his brother Jerol in a car dealership in Covington and later owned his own car dealership as well. He was also a member of the Tennessee National Guard and had been flying since 1973. After returning from a tour of duty in Iraq, he decided to buy a helicopter for himself and fly just for the fun of it.

I should not have been surprised by anything that Mike Hopkins did. When he was in my sixth grade, he overheard my conversation with another teacher as I told her that Bill and I were about to buy a new, blue Chevrolet. Mike's brother was already in the business of selling Fords in

Covington, so Mike piped up and said, "No ma'am! You're not going to buy a Chevrolet, Miss Vivian! You're going to buy a new Ford from me!"

I was surprised by his comment and responded, "But, Mike, my husband and I have already decided on the blue Chevy."

Mike insisted. "Give me a chance to bring you some information about buying a Ford from my brother. You won't be sorry."

I was intrigued by this sixth-grade boy's initiative and determination, so I agreed and said, "O.K., Mike, let's see what you can do."

The very next day, Mike came to school with pamphlets and papers. He showed me a photo of a beautiful maroon Ford, and, with a salesman's enthusiasm, explained what it would cost us and how much money he could save us. He did a very thorough job of making his case, and I agreed to take the papers home and share them with Bill.

Of course, Bill went over Mike's information in great detail, as he always did when making a big decision. He had some questions, so he called Mike and got his answers. The next day, we drove to Covington and spoke with Mike's brother Jerol and decided to buy the pretty maroon Ford. We were happy because we got a great deal, and Mike was happy because he had sold his first car. In return for his efforts, Mike earned $100 and a pig!

So, years later, during that drop-in visit in my "outdoor parlor," Mike and I relived the sixth-grade car sale and shared some good laughs. We reminisced about the crazy overnight adventure when he and a bunch of boys from my sixth-grade class spent a night camping in borrowed Boy Scout tents in our side yard. He even remembered that the next day they played ball in the very same pasture where he landed his helicopter—and he chuckled that they had to dodge a few cow patties on their makeshift ballfield!

Finally, Mike headed back to his helicopter, but not before promising to come back and take me for my first helicopter ride.

Did I tell you that I love surprises?

Grunt, the Party Animal

As I was growing up in the town of Brighton, we always raised a couple of hogs that eventually turned into wonderful pork, ham, and bacon for our winter table. One year, the mother hog died while delivering her litter. That left us with five little piglets to nurture. We fed them cow's milk in bottles with regular baby nipples. We were disappointed that most of the babies did not survive. Later, we learned from the veterinarian that, in its natural state, cow's milk was too rich for the tiny piglets and that we probably should have diluted it. All but one of the orphans died. Needless to say, that one surviving piglet became very special to us.

Our little survivor became a pet in the Baird household. I do not remember who named him, but we all called him by the elegant name, "Grunt," which, we figured, was a name that other pigs could also pronounce.

Daddy built a pig pen in the backyard using hog wire designed for the purpose, but Grunt was not so easily controlled. He quickly and repeatedly dug his way under the side of the pen and would be found wandering freely around the yard. When we wanted to get him back into the pen, we

would first have to fill the hole that he had dug, then play a
trick to lure him back inside. This was not too difficult. Once
the hole was filled, we would grab the feeding pail and bang
on it with a stick or tool. Being a pig and always ready to eat,
he would think it was feeding time. He would promptly
report back to the pen and to the feeding trough—and we
would quickly close and lock the gate behind him!

Grunt was very friendly and would allow us to pet his dark
red hair. He became so socialized that he did not like being
outside by himself, and he eventually learned how to let
himself into the house where people were.

Our house had a wooden screen door that opened onto the
screened-in back porch. This door could be secured by a
simple hook and eye that was usually left unhooked. Grunt
learned that by repeatedly bumping the unlatched screen
door with his snout, he could cause the screen door to
bounce open just enough that he could catch the side of the
door with his snout and let himself into the porch and then
into the house through the hall! On his own, he would come
casually walking through the house looking for someone to
pet him.

Grunt was quite tame, and he wanted to be where the
people were. One hot August when Rudy was sitting on the
front porch with a group of friends who had come to help
him celebrate his birthday, they heard this mysterious
bumping noise coming from the back area of the house.
When the friends wondered about the noise, Rudy assured
them that it was nothing to worry about. The bumping
continued… They decided to investigate. Sure enough,

when Rudy and his friends went inside to check it out, they found Grunt wandering through the house looking for the party!

Eventually, it came time for Grunt to fulfill his life's mission and provide food for the Baird table. Mother could not be a part of it. She went away from the house for the entire day so that she did not have to be a part of Grunt's demise. She also could not eat any of the meat that came from Grunt. In her eyes—and her heart—he had become too much a part of the family for that.

Part Five
Vivian Grows Up

Vivian, circa 1938

My Long-Distance Friend

While I was in the eleventh grade at Brighton High School, our church—the Brighton Associate Reformed Presbyterian—was the host for the annual meeting of our denomination's Young People's Christian Union (YPCU). Members came to Brighton from Tennessee, Arkansas, Missouri, and Mississippi. They stayed for several days in the homes of host families from the church and participated in picnics, classes, field trips, and many games.

During this meeting, I became friends with a young man named Paul Keaton from Russellville, Arkansas. During the following year, Paul and I corresponded regularly, but did not see each other again until the next year's YPCU meeting, which was held in Missouri. Following this second meeting, we continued to write and call one another regularly, but, we did not meet again until the next year when the meeting was hosted by Paul's home church in Russellville.

During that meeting, Paul was not able to be with us all of the time because of his work schedule, but he did spend most afternoons with the group. Paul had a new car at the time, and it was the first car I remember that had the gear shift on the steering column instead of coming up out of the floor. He and his new car with the gear shift on the steering column were the center of attention! I especially remember a great picnic that the group had at the Petite Jean Mountain State Park when everyone was intrigued by the new car. Paul even allowed me to drive it from the park to the home of the host family where I was staying. Another driving adventure for me—but this time, it was legal!

After that summer, Paul drove the 240 miles from Russellville to Brighton several times to visit. On one visit, he flew his own plane from Russellville and landed at a small airfield near Millington. My friend Anna Lucado and I drove to the airfield to meet him and to give him a ride to a Covington hotel where he would stay. This time, his airplane was the center of our attention. I remember getting on the plane and Paul explaining everything to me. It was not until I contacted Paul's son in my later years and following Paul's death that I found out that he had built that plane himself from a kit. He must have done a good job because he flew everywhere in that plane!

One other lasting memory from Paul sits in my house to this day and does whatever I ask of it. When I was still in my junior year at Memphis State Teachers College, I received a letter from Paul advising me to expect a surprise gift in the mail. He told me that it was something that he had made, but he offered no other clues about it.

One day in October 1937, my dorm-mates and I had gathered for our daily mail call on the first floor of Mynders Hall. Mrs. Harper, the dorm mother and perhaps the meanest woman that ever walked the earth, called my name and commented that she had a very heavy package for me. "What could be in this?" she asked.

This special package caught the attention of all of the other girls. The box was not very big, but it sure was heavy for its size. Everyone started to chant, "Open it! Open it! Open it!" What could I do? I *had* to open it…

I unwrapped the package and discovered that I was now the proud owner of an iron frog! It was about the size of a small cantaloupe and really, really heavy.

Within the box was a hand-written note that read as follows:

> *Please take care of my Paul, the Frog*
> *He will hold your papers down*
> *He will hold your door open*
> *Just tell him what to do and he will do*
> *whatever you ask…just like the one who made him.*

I found out later that Paul, using the tools of his father's blacksmith shop and the skills he had picked up working with his father, had made this frog from an old railroad track. The iron frog has been my faithful servant for the past seventy-plus years. He still sits in our living room, holding open the door to our "nest." Since then, I have never been without him or without memories of his maker.

Storms and Panic:
Natural and Girl-Made

In 1936, Helen DeWese and I were students at Memphis State Teachers College, now the University of Memphis. Many weekends, we went home to Brighton to be with family and friends. On Sunday evenings, my boyfriend Bill (Winfield McLennan) and Helen's boyfriend Milton Simonton— the two men we would eventually marry— would drive us back to college. Our goal was to arrive just in time to beat the Sunday evening curfew, which was diligently enforced by Mrs. Harper, referred to *lovingly* by most of the girls as the "witch." In making our timing calculations, we always built in time for our usual stop at the Pig N'Whistle for a barbeque sandwich and ice cream, requirements for our Sunday evening trips.

One Sunday that spring, our routine changed when Bill's parents, Dan and Bertie McLennan, invited Bill and me to have the evening meal with them before we headed back to Memphis. Just after we finished our supper, Mr. Dan noticed that the sky was darkening in a menacing way. He checked the radio and learned that a tornado was heading in our direction. It was following a frequently traveled storm track

from Oklahoma, through Arkansas and Tennessee, on its
way east, a storm path known as Tornado Alley. This time,
the sky to our west was an eerie yellowish-pink color and
growing very dark and threatening.

Drawing upon his years of observing weather and Mother
Nature, Mr. Dan decided, much to my chagrin, that it was
time for us to retreat to their storm cellar. This was a safe
underground bunker built by farmers and homeowners as a
retreat to protect them and their families from destruction
caused by severe storms and tornados. Many of these
underground rooms doubled as root cellars as well.

The typical storm cellar was a dugout room with a short
concrete wall extending about two feet above ground. The
roof of the cellar was also concrete and very flat. The floor
and the interior walls of the enclosure were compacted dirt
reinforced by wood or concrete. The interior height of the
room was usually over six feet and the entrance, which was
at ground level on the outside, was two-thirds of the way up
to the ceiling on the inside.

The McLennan's storm cellar was tall enough for my six-
foot-tall boyfriend Bill, to stand up inside it. Their family
also used it as a root cellar for storing their home-canned
goods as well as fresh fruits and vegetables they had grown.
It even contained chairs for the comfort of those who had to
stay in the shelter for any length of time, and there was a
lantern for light. A wooden box made by Bill's Uncle Harry,
who was Miss Bertie's brother, stayed in the cellar to help
people step up to the level of the exit when it was time to get
out. There was also a fruit jar that held candles, matches,

and a whistle. The whistle was to aid rescuers if the cellar was ever covered with debris from a tornado.

A hinged door covered the opening to the storm cellar and opened to the outside, but it did not fit snugly. This was the source of my main concern about the storm cellar. When I had previously looked at the opening, I could see plenty of opportunities for snakes and other "varmints" to get inside. When I thought of having to go into the cellar myself, I shuddered at the prospect of sharing space with these other critters which, I imagined, overpopulated the space.

After several loud claps of thunder and nearby bolts of lightning, Mr. Dan told Bill, "Take Bertie and Vivian into the cellar. This is going to be a bad one."

Pretending to be brave, I said to Bill, "I'd rather *not* go into the cellar. I'll stay here."

Bill ignored my protest, saying, "Come on. We're heading in."

Miss Bertie and I followed Bill out of the dining room, through the kitchen, and out the east door onto the porch. We went out through the screen door, stepped down onto a brick walkway, turned left, walked west past the pump house on the right, and across the grass to the storm cellar—all of this as the fierce storm swirled around us.

Now that we were outside, I suddenly appreciated how threatening the storm was and why Mr. Dan was worried. Lightning was flashing, thunder was booming, and rain was starting to come down. Suddenly, I was frightened by the storm—but I was even more frightened by the storm cellar!

Following his dad's orders, Bill went ahead of us and opened the storm cellar door. He sat down on the ground and slid feet first down into the cellar so that he could help those of us who were considerably shorter. Miss Bertie sat down and slid in feet first just as Bill did. I held back a little, trying not to show my fear. Bill called to me firmly, "*Just sit down and slide in!*"

I did not want to go down into that "cave," but the storm was looming. I tried not to show my fear as I sat on the ground and slid forward into the opening. Bill caught me and helped me down to the floor. We lit the lantern, but kept the door ajar to monitor the storm. I was deeply relieved that the bunker harbored no critters but us!

Mr. Dan stayed up in the yard to keep an eye on the tornado. Occasionally, he would come over near the cellar and holler down to us, "Are y'all alright?" Then he would go back into the house to the telephone trying to reach his sister, Aunt Maude, and her husband, Uncle Jim Anthony, and other family members. His calls were fruitless, either because the lines were down or the party lines were being used by other neighbors trying to locate their family members. As the tornado drew closer, Mr. Dan stayed near the back door of the house and within running distance of the cellar until the high winds and strong rains eased.

After the tornado had passed, Mr. Dan walked through to the front of the house to look for any damage. When he got to the front room, he received a big surprise. Sitting there in his "nest" were family friends, Mr. and Mrs. Lucian Liles and their four children! He also found two of his hired farmhands, Ossie and Pearl, sitting there talking to the Liles family. Apparently, while we had evacuated the house for the protection of the storm cellar, these folks came to the McLennan's house thinking that it would be safer than their own. Mr. Dan, who had stayed near the back of the house to keep an eye on us in the storm cellar, never heard them come in and was shocked to find that these unexpected-but-welcome guests had made themselves at home!

Mr. Dan returned to the backyard to announce to us in the storm cellar that the storm had eased and that we had visitors. We climbed out of the bunker and made our way to the living room to share excited observations about what we had all just experienced. Eventually, the guests headed home to check on their own houses.

Shortly afterward, Helen and Milton arrived to pick up Bill and me to go back to Memphis State. Mr. Dan was worried about the storm's aftermath and was not at all happy about our heading to Memphis so soon following the tornado. He tried every which way to convince us to stay overnight at their house until we could be sure that the storms had passed and the roads were clear. But Helen and I felt that we really had to get back to school. She was scheduled for a violin performance the next day, and I had a history test.

The four of us headed directly to Memphis State without our customary stop at the Pig'n Whistle. When we arrived at the dormitory, we learned that there on campus, the storm was much less severe so Mrs. Harper was not willing to acknowledge what we had just been through. She came at us in her typical nasty manner, angrily demanding to know why we were late. With Helen in the lead, we tried to explain, but Mrs. Harper did not have an empathetic bone in her body. She finally allowed us to go to the door to say good-bye to Milton and Bill, but warned us that we were not to go outside. We resented her attitude, but went to our rooms convinced that the next day's news would vindicate our late return.

Perhaps it was the excitement of the tornado or the boiling over of months of resentment toward Mrs. Harper's iron hand that led a group of girls to create a storm of our own. Word passed quietly from room to room throughout the dorm that, at the stroke of midnight, each one of us would slam our door as loud as we could. Because I had a history test the next day, I was up studying later than usual. When I was done studying, I decided to walk down the hall and take a shower before turning in. Just as I stepped out of the shower, the clock struck 12:00, and nearly every door in the building slammed. It sounded like the dormitory had exploded!

I quickly put on my robe and headed back to my room, dripping all the way. Just as I passed the stairwell, a few feet before my room, I encountered Mrs. Harper coming up the stairs. She looked fit to be tied. Her face was as red as her flaming hair.

She hollered at me, "What are you doing?"

I stammered, "I was just taking a shower."

She bellowed, "Who else was in on this? Everyone come to my room!"

All the girls, dressed in their robes, pajamas, and slippers, moved down the stairs. All except me. I was shivering in just my robe…and still dripping. The girls were filling the hall and *innocently* asking each other *"What happened?" "What caused that awful noise?"*

Dr. Nellie Angel Smith, who was in charge of the women's dormitory and lived in our building, also appeared in the hallway. She demanded, "Who did that?" No one seemed to know what caused the Big Bang. Some muttered that it was most likely the wind and weather that caused the doors to slam. Nobody squealed.

While they grilled us, I was still in my bathrobe, still barefooted, and getting colder by the second. I felt like I needed some help so I spoke up and asked Dr. Smith if I could be excused to get my clothes. At that point, she dismissed everyone.

As I returned to my room, I was amazed to find my roommate, Vivian Taylor, still sound asleep in her bed. She had slept through all of the fun and noise of our homemade storm!

In the morning, even though we had experienced the raging storm and winds ourselves, we were shocked to learn about the extensive damage the tornados had done in Brighton,

Clopton, Salem, Rosemark, and other areas north of Memphis. The greatest damage in the area was in Tupelo, Mississippi, which was practically destroyed. The storm spawned twelve separate tornados and came to be known as the Tupelo-Gainesville Outbreak. While it centered around Tupelo, Mississippi, and then on to Gainesville, Georgia, extensive damage was reported in Arkansas, Tennessee, Mississippi, Alabama, Georgia, and South Carolina. Records show that, across these states, 454 people were killed and countless homes and businesses destroyed.

Later that day I told my friends, Street and Chapman, about the midnight excitement, but it was not news to them. They'd already heard about the girl-made "storm over the dorm"!

Vivian and the Depression: "Making Ends Meet"

The Great Depression was still a looming factor when I went to college in 1935. Daddy was able to pay for my tuition for my first year, but when I was about to begin my fall term at Memphis State in September 1936, Daddy let me know that he would not be able to afford the tuition for that year. It was a sit-out year for me.

In an effort to help out financially, I first took a job at "The Greasy Spoon," a small restaurant in town. It was on a street corner near the high school. I worked there in the mornings helping out in the kitchen and cleaning up the restaurant. By 1:00 P.M., I was done at "The Spoon," and had some time on my hands.

Around that time, I heard that Mr. Leno and Miss Mildred Morrison were looking for someone to help them with their laundry. I went to them and asked if they would trust me to do that for them. They thought that I could handle that job, so it gave me a new idea for a business. I decided to move boldly on this idea. So, as a college freshman, I went into Memphis, bought a washing machine at Stratton-Warren

Wholesale Hardware Store, and charged it to the Baird Brothers Hardware. Then I went to Daddy's store and told him what I had done. I offered to pay for the washing machine with the money I made from doing laundry. He agreed that this was a good idea, and I set off to recruit more customers. Eventually, I kept between five and ten families as customers and made enough money to pay for the washing machine and save for college so I could return to Memphis State.

Later I heard from Daddy that my Uncle Ben Fortner, who ran a blacksmith shop in Covington, was looking for some help with his bookkeeping. I went to visit Uncle Ben, offered my services, and he offered me the job. After trying to do the work at Uncle Ben's shop, I found that it was too noisy and dirty for me to concentrate. At first, Uncle Ben and Aunt Jenny, my dad's sister, allowed me to take the books over to their house and work there. Later they allowed me to do it at our own home.

Between the income I earned from being a "laundress" and the bookkeeping work for the blacksmith shop, I earned enough money to pay my next year's tuition. In 1937, I returned to Memphis State and continued my education and my dream of becoming a teacher.

Burlison Days

In January, 1938, after "sitting out" for over a year to earn tuition money, I returned to the State Teachers College in Memphis for the second term of my Junior year. School was not as much fun as it had been earlier because my good friend Helen DeWese and her roommate Frances Strong had graduated the previous spring, and I really missed them. I especially missed Frances because she went over every English paper I turned in, and her expertise really helped my English grades!

The country was still caught up in the Great Depression. Everyone was struggling to make ends meet, and paying college tuition was very difficult for most people, including Daddy. Like many of my peers, I looked around at what was going on, and I felt that I had to do my part to help my family.

For all of these reasons, I used a part of my semester and holiday break from college to visit the Tipton County Superintendent of Schools, Mr. Younger. At that time, to be hired as a teacher, a person only had to have completed one year of college. Since I was already in my Junior year, I was more than qualified. My conversation with Mr. Younger was very encouraging. I was especially filled with hope when, at the close of our interview, he said, "The county would be very happy to have you as a teacher." I left his office feeling that before the new school year began in July, I would know if I were to have a job as a teacher.

For now, I was back in college. My roommate, Vivian Taylor, and I settled in quickly. I had registered and lined up good used textbooks for all of my classes and was happy to be back with my friends. On my first evening back on campus, my two "boy buddies," Calvin Street and Wilder Chapman, came by to welcome me back. I had worked in the cafeteria with the two of them, and we had formed a special bond. Some of us who worked in the cafeteria would frequently go to the movie theater together after our work shift. We grew to be very good friends.

It took me a little while to learn the location of my new classes that semester. I remember sitting in one class for about ten minutes before realizing that I was in the wrong class! A few days into the new semester, I was sitting in class when another student walked in and handed me a note. The note read, "Call the Superintendent of Schools in Covington."

I became very excited! "What was this about? Is there a job for me?" I was so excited that I got up and walked out of class without saying anything to the professor. I needed to make a long distance call from Memphis to Covington, and I had no money with me. I ran all the way back to my dormitory and retrieved enough money to return the call.

At that time, married ladies were not permitted to teach in the public schools. I did not realize it then, but married women were not permitted to teach because of the fear that their working would take a job from a man who was expected to be the bread winner for the family.

When I got Mr. Younger on the phone, he told me that one of his teachers, Frances Kelly, had married during the Christmas vacation and that he was looking for a replacement. Mr. Younger was asking me to consider replacing Miss Kelly as a teacher at Burlison School!

Burlison was a small community west of Brighton, nearer the Mississippi River. Mr. Younger suggested I go to visit Mr. Edgar Glover who was the Principal at Burlison Elementary. The next day, Mother drove to the college in Memphis to pick me up. On our way home, she made it clear that it was entirely my own decision whether I would begin teaching right away or complete my college school year first. We also discussed my interview with Mr. Glover and whether she should accompany me. We decided that it would be best if I went to the interview by myself. I dropped Mother off at our home in Brighton and then used her car to continue on to Burlison to meet with Mr. Glover.

Ed Glover and his family lived across the road from the school. I called on him there, and, after he welcomed me warmly, we went across the road to look at the school building. The school was a white wooden building with four classrooms and a small room called the music room. Just inside the entry, there were two sets of stairs that led to the large classrooms and the music room. Underneath each stairway was a cloak room where the students and the staff hung their coats in cold weather. Mr. Glover showed me the downstairs classrooms. On the right side was the classroom for the first and second grades. Mr. Glover told me that Miss Eloise Huffman was the teacher in that room. When we turned to the left side, he said, "This will be your classroom, Miss Baird. It will be third and fourth graders." I was surprised, but I began to feel that this was what I wanted to do.

We also took a look at the two classrooms upstairs. On one side of the second floor was the music room. Across the hall, there were two doors. One was for the fifth and sixth grades, and the other was for the seventh and eighth grades. Mable Shankle was the teacher for the fifth and sixth grades, and her room had been extended on the west side to permit the addition of a stage. Mr. Glover himself was the teacher of the seventh and eighth grade classes and was also the basketball coach.

After an opportunity to ask Mr. Glover all the questions I could think of, I told him that I thought I would like to accept the offer and be the teacher for the third and fourth grades at Burlison. He felt that he would have no difficulty convincing Mr. Younger that I should be formally offered the job. I left feeling that I was on the right path.

When I knew that I was coming home for the interview, I also made an appointment to have my hair washed and set at the Crescent Beauty Parlor on the town square in Covington. When I left Mr. Glover, I headed directly to the beauty parlor. I was so excited that Mr. Glover seemed so positive that I would be offered the job that I could not contain myself. Naturally, I had to tell everyone at the beauty parlor about my exciting good news.

Then, I got the shock of my life! Miss Mildred, the owner of the beauty parlor, asked incredulously, *"Are you really going to teach at Burlison?"* Then she explained why she asked. *"My mother taught there once, and one afternoon some of the big boys in the school nailed the door shut while she was in the music room and then they all went home."*

Of course, I thought she was just teasing me—but then one of the other customers spoke up saying, *"My mother taught at Burlison, and one day the big boys tied her to a tree and left!"*

I could not believe what I was hearing. "I know," I insisted, "you are just teasing me." They insisted just as strongly that they were telling the truth.

As soon as I left the beauty parlor, I drove back to Burlison and went directly to Mr. Glover's house. I told him about what had happened at the beauty parlor, and I asked him about the stories I had heard.

Mr. Glover sighed and shook his head like a man who had heard it all before. Then he spoke.

"Yes," he said, "things like that used to happen here. But that was a while ago. In the four years I have been here, nothing like that has happened. The students and their parents have been very supportive, and you will never find nicer people."

Despite the warnings in the beauty shop, I took the job immediately without returning to Memphis State classes and found out for myself that Mr. Glover was correct. I taught the third and fourth grades there for three years. The salary was $55 per month, but the county even had difficulty paying that small amount. Instead of a pay check, there were many months when teachers just got a "warrant." This was a formal process by which the county promised to pay you a certain amount of money, once the money became available. It was understood that when money became available, the warrants would be redeemed in the date and time order in which they had been registered.

Mr. Glover wanted us to get our money just as soon as it was available, so on the last day of each pay period, he would ask one of the other teachers or a former teacher to stay with his students so that he could deliver our pay vouchers to the county office as early as possible. Once the vouchers were recorded and the warrants issued, Mr. Glover would then have to take the warrants to the County Courthouse to have them registered. Because of his willingness to go this extra mile, we Burlison teachers often received our pay long before others who did not have such thoughtful administrators.

During my years at Burlison, I became really involved with the community. During the Depression, a large room was built onto the back of the school building. It had a kitchen at one end and a dining area at the other. This was a part of a national effort to make sure that children received proper nutrition during those difficult times when many families went hungry. Children were provided a nutritious and warm lunch so that they would receive at least one good meal a day. The charge was three cents a day—if they could afford it. The kitchen at Burlison was also open to the parents and to other adults in the community who were having difficulty getting enough food to survive. Many of these adults who ate at the school contributed in-kind services in exchange for their meals and the meals of their children.

I especially remember one father of some of our students, Mr. Will Lowery, who often came for lunch. In exchange, he would do yard work around the school grounds.He had the longest beard that I had ever seen, and one day I asked him about it. He told me that he had grown his beard in protest to his wife's cutting her hair short!

Mr. Lowery was also the unwitting author of an expression that became quite a cliché in our family. After eating lunch at the school one day, he pushed back from the table, rubbed his stomach appreciatively, and announced, *"I wouldn't a been any fuller if I'd 'et at the Peabody!"* This expression has been quoted innumerable times over the years around the Baird and McLennan tables!

I also began to notice that many of our children would walk to school, regardless of the weather or the warmth of their clothes. This was especially noticeable during the rainy season when the children would show up at the school door with very muddy shoes from the dirt roads that they had to walk in order to get to school. Eventually, I was able to provide a couple of large brown mats at the door for the children to use. I was always proud to look at the mats and read the wording on them: "Baird Brothers Hardware Store."

I was surprised to learn that the well that served the school had gone dry. In order to provide the children with a little water for drinking, two students from each classroom would take that room's water bucket and walk about a quarter mile to Mr. Dawson's house to draw buckets of water from his well. When they brought the buckets back to their classrooms, they would put the room's two dippers into the bucket, and the children would use a dipper to help themselves to a drink whenever they needed one—or wash their hands in the bucket of water. I was appalled at this unsanitary practice, and I asked my boyfriend, Bill McLennan, to help me develop a solution.

Bill, a gifted craftsman, got busy. First, he built a table that was about waist high for the students. He then cut a hole in the table large enough for a metal hand-washing basin. He cut a hole in the center of a basin and soldered a funnel onto the bottom of it, around the hole. From the spout of the funnel, he ran a hose down to a small hole he cut into the floor. He fed the hose through the hole, creating a drain from the wash basin through the floor and onto the ground below the classroom. After we installed Bill's creation, the students brought the water from Mr. Dawson's well and placed the bucket on the table beside their new "sink." At last, they had a place to wash their hands without contaminating the drinking water!

Bill also built a cabinet beside the new makeshift sink. I had gone to Daddy's store and obtained a tin cup for each student in the class. I brought them to the school and put a child's name on each cup. Then each child was assigned a space in the cabinet for his or her cup. Now, with Bill's help and skill, the water brought from Mr. Dawson's well was available for sanitary drinking.

Finally, the arrangement that Bill had built provided an opportunity to wash the cups each week. Eventually, I found a way to heat the water, and we were able to wash the cups in hot water and kill off a few more germs.

Every Friday, I would ask the students to write an original story using the week's spelling words. Somehow, one of the students, Eugene Roberts, always included in his stories that he was riding his "pouney." Of course, I would remind him every week that "pony" was spelled "p-o-n-y." The next week, he would again spell it "p-o-u-n-e-y." While engaging in this ongoing spelling battle with Eugene, I realized that he did, in fact, ride his pony to school every day. I also realized that he rode along a part of the route that I drove between Burlison and Brighton. One day I asked him, "Do you prefer to ride your pony to school or would you rather ride in my car?" Not surprisingly, he said that he would rather ride in the car. This was the beginning of my using Daddy's 1937 Ford to pick up some of the children who were walking along the same route I was driving. First there was Eugene, then there was a little girl who lived far off the main highway down a country road. And finally I began to pick up the Lowery kids—and there were a lot of them! Daddy's 1937 Ford was packed to the gills, and it groaned its way to Burlison School most mornings and then back again in the afternoon!

It was also the custom in the Burlison area for the families of the students to extend hospitality to the school's teachers.

Many families would invite one or two of the teachers to dinner and then provide them a place to stay the night. We really got to know our students and their families, and the people of Burlison helped us teachers feel like an important part of their community.

Perhaps these special touches that so effectively tied the teachers of Burlison School to the community were responsible for my getting a telephone call in the 1990s from Buford Walker, one of my former Burlison students. He told me that several of the "children" that I had taught while at Burlison, had begun to meet once a month to have lunch together and to talk about the fun they had while in school. One of the participants observed that they badly needed a teacher to make them behave, and someone suggested that they call "Miss Vivian," to be their disciplinarian!

This monthly gathering continued a long and very pleasant re-association with my "Burlison children." Many thanks to one of those "children," Martha Jean Goulder, who graciously served as my chauffeur for years after my macular degeneration prevented me from driving.

I have enjoyed telling people about getting together once a month with my "children." Then, when they begin to hear those stories, they would often ask, "So...*how old are these children?*" I enjoy watching their expressions when I nonchalantly tell them, "*Oh, about seventy-five.*"

Clearly, Mr. Glover was right. The Burlison community introduced me to some of the nicest people that I have ever met.

Teaching in Tipton

After I had taught third and fourth grades for three years at Burlison Elementary School, I was offered an opportunity to move to a teaching position in Brighton. It was difficult for me to think about leaving Burlison. I had become very attached to the children and to the entire community there, but Brighton was home. I had attended Brighton School myself from first grade to the twelfth grade, and I was excited at the thought of going back to teach at my old school. The move to Brighton also fit in with my personal plans. I was engaged to Winfield Brown McLennan, whom everyone called "Bill," and we were to be married on October 9, 1941. Our plan was to live in the Clopton community near Brighton.

It is interesting to note that my opportunity to teach at Burlison came because the teacher I replaced had gotten married, and at that time, married women were not permitted to teach in the public schools. However, by 1941, three years later, this policy had changed; married women were now allowed to teach, so I could marry Bill and teach, too!

By the time the school bell rang to open the 1941-42 school year, I was assigned to teach the second grade children at Brighton School. I taught there for three years until the end of the school year in the spring of 1944. At that time, I was pregnant and looking forward to the birth of our daughter, Mary Nelle, in December.

I spent the next five years helping Mary Nelle get started in life and beginning her school years. After surviving the death of our second child who died at birth when Mary Nelle was five years old, I began to feel that I needed more day-to-day stimulation and interest in my life. Bill went to work each day and Mary Nelle went to school, and I had a lot of time on my hands.

One day, I went to visit my good friend, Clara McMillan, who worked in the County Court Clerk's Office, assisting Mr. Henry Vaughn, the elected County Court Clerk of Tipton County. Clara and I had met and become friends when we both served as counselors in the Methodist Youth Fellowship (MYF). As Clara and I were sitting in her office chatting, Mr. Vaughn himself came in and said hello. He seemed to know more about me than I had expected, and he mentioned that he knew I had been a teacher at Brighton. Much to my surprise, he asked if I might be interested in a clerk's job in his office!

This was an intriguing option for me and raised my curiosity. I did not think I was ready to work again, but here was a job that had fallen into my lap. When I went home, I was eager to get Bill's reaction to this offer. In his typical droll response, he said, "If I told you to take the job, you could say that I told you to go to work. If I said, 'don't take it,' you could say that I would not let you go to work." In other words, he was saying, "You can do whatever you want to do." It was my decision to make.

When the day came for me to visit Mr. Vaughn's office and let him know my decision, I walked into the office not really knowing what I was going to say. After talking with him and discussing it further, I felt good about it and said, "Yes, I'll try to do this job."

The job was interesting and fun. While working in this public place, I had an opportunity to see many of my school children and their families from Burlison and from Brighton. I enjoyed being with people again. I was still getting over the death of our son, and I found that spending too much time home alone had not been good. And I enjoyed being with my friend Clara every day.

I had begun working in February, and things moved along smoothly until one summer day when Mr. McClanahan, the Superintendent of the Tipton County Schools, came into the office. He saw me sitting there typing and remarked on the fact that as a trained teacher, I should be in the classroom. I told him that I liked this job, that I got paid directly for the hours that I worked, and that Mr. Vaughn had said that if I needed to take time off to be with Mary Nelle, my work would be waiting for me when I got back. This seemed to be what I needed at that time, so I thanked Mr. McClanahan for the compliment and went on about my business.

But Mr. McClanahan was persistent. He came back several times and talked to me about returning to teaching. Again, I thanked him and told him I was happy working as a clerk in the court house. Then one day, he came back with Albert Kelly, the Principal of Holmes Elementary School in Covington. Now they were double-teaming me!

Even Mr. Vaughn joined in on the conversation, and he seemed to be supportive in saying that he could understand that I might want to return to teaching. Mr. McLenahan and Mr. Kelly told me about a specific opening for a first-grade teacher at Holmes School. Mr. Kelly met me after work one day and took me to Holmes to show me the actual classroom where I would be teaching if I took the position.

I began to think that I would really like to return to teaching and being with children, but I had not yet made up my mind. Of course, I was flattered to have these top administrators pursuing me and trying to convince me to teach again. That evening, I discussed it all with Bill and made the decision to give it a try.

On my very first day as a teacher at Holmes School, as I was getting to know my new students, I was surprised by the sound of light tapping on the window of my classroom door. I went to the door and found Mr. J. H. Bennett, the Principal of Brighton School. Much to my surprise, he had stopped by to tell me that he had a last minute opening for a teacher at his school and that the School Superintendent had given him permission to offer me the job. Of course, I was wishing that I could return to Brighton, but I felt that I could not leave these new first graders whom I had just met for the first time.

I told Mr. Bennett that while I was flattered by his offer, I felt that I had accepted the position at Holmes and that I should stay here for the year.

My year at Holmes Elementary was very pleasant. I have many wonderful memories of the people and my time there!

One of the other Holmes teachers was Frances Slover whom I had met as a fellow teacher during my original years as a teacher in Brighton. Frances lived at Mt. Carmel, which was half-way from my house in Clopton to Holmes School in Covington. We took turns driving to school. Every other week, I would drive all the way to Covington and pick up Frances on the way. On the opposite weeks, I would drive to her home in Mt. Carmel and leave my car there as Frances would drive us to Covington in her car.

Early in the year, I remember the mother of one of my new students telling me a funny anecdote. She had brought her son to the school for the initial registration and to meet some of the teachers. After the first day of school, the mother asked her son who his new teacher was. He said, "Well, it was not the old woman, and it was not the teacher in the middle room, it was the fat woman in the green dress." That was me!

Another student named Jimmy asked permission one day to bring his pet blackbird to school. The bird's name was "Blackberry," and Jimmy wanted to show it to his classmates. I agreed to Blackberry's visit, and we kept him at school for a few days. The students learned how to feed Blackberry and care for him. It was a good learning experience for everyone.

A few years later, I received a note from the student in his own hand-writing saying very succinctly, "Dear Miss Vivian, Blackberry is dead. Love, Jimmy."

After school was out for the summer that year, I had gathered one day to go fishing with a few of my friends—Elizabeth Huffman, Jean Hill Chisolm, Ada Rose Anthony, and Helen Simonton. First we tried Cousin Mildred McLennan's pond off Poindexter Road. After we caught a few nice fish there, we decided to try our luck fishing in the slough which ran along side McLennan Road. At that time, the slough was filled with several feet of water and plenty of fish.

Just as we had decided that it was not a good day for fishing in the slough and were getting ready to leave, a car passed by heading west toward my house. A few minutes later, we saw the same car return, slow down, and come to a stop near where we were packing up our fishing gear. We all recognized Mr. Bennett as he got out of the car and came walking toward us. He said, "Oh, there you are, Vivian. I just went to your house looking for you, and I just happened to see you all here as I was driving back by." He went on to say, "I have good news for you. We have another opening at Brighton School for next year, and I wondered if you might like to apply." Once again, a job had come looking for me!

The next day, I went to the office of the Superintendent of Schools and submitted my application. Soon I was notified that my application had been accepted, and I would again teach at Brighton School. When I stopped by the school to follow up with Mr. Bennett, he showed me to the room and announced with a laugh, "This is the same old room where you taught in 1944, but we gave you a new coat of paint!"

I began my second tenure of teaching at Brighton School in the first grade. It was a successful year, and I learned a lot. The next year, and for a few after that, I stayed in that same room, but this time it was with second grade children. As the next school year was beginning and I had gathered with the other teachers for the opening day of in-service training, Mr. Bennett approached me and asked, "How do you feel about teaching sixth graders?" I told him, "I'll do my best," and I did for the next six years and enjoyed every one of them.

Then, during the opening day in-service of the following school year, Mr. Bennett approached and asked me, "How do you feel about fourth graders?" This time I was not as open to the change at first. I told him, "I would rather stay with the sixth grade." But Mr. Bennett let me know that he really wanted me to switch to the fourth grade.

As I thought about it, I decided that the fourth graders I had known were smart enough to enjoy learning and had also developed a sense of humor, and so I decided to agree to Mr. Bennett's request. I happily taught fourth graders for the next twenty years until I retired in 1980.

The sixth grade social studies curriculum included a long unit on American history. That was right down my alley and allowed me to share my interest in antiques and the history of our country with my students.

I had been collecting antiques since my childhood and had developed quite a collection of my own. I began to bring some of my old items into school to share with the children and to try to bring their lessons to life. I shared with them a spinning wheel that I owned and an old-fashioned butter churn, and I showed how they had been used. I brought in some very old books, scrapbooks of faded photos from the 1800s, and handwritten letters that were characteristic of the times we were discussing. I displayed and demonstrated different types of lanterns and tools, various farming implements and plows, and a wall-mounted crank telephone to name a few.

What was surprising about this teaching approach and what made it very special was that, as I began to bring these items to class, the students began to tell about objects their families had and even brought in old things that their parents or grandparents had saved or collected. This not only added to the number and variety of antiques that the students had a chance to learn about, but it also provided an opportunity for the children to talk about these things with members of their family and to appreciate some of their own family's history.

Before I knew it, we had our own little museum for a few weeks each year. In addition to the hardware, we had all sorts of clothing representing many different time periods in our country. I even had a stove pipe hat like Abraham Lincoln's and some big petticoats like those worn by women of that time. The students dressed in period costume and developed presentations about the eras they represented.

One item the students found most interesting was my husband's grandfather's civil war uniform. He was a soldier in the Confederate Army, and the uniform even had a bullet hole where he had been wounded in battle. The opportunity to wear the soldier's uniform was the subject of a special lottery each year. The name of every child who wanted to wear the uniform was entered into the contest and one name was drawn. The winner had an opportunity to play a special role in that year's antique show and open house.

The antique shows took on a life of their own. Word spread about the variety of items on display. Soon we opened it to the public, welcoming guests from the community, explaining the items on display, and of course, serving refreshments. For many years, our Antiques Show and Open House was covered in the news by *The Covington Leader* and by the *Commercial Appeal* in Memphis.

Finally, in 1981, after thirty-five years in the classroom, it came time to retire. Having taught for so many years in Tipton County provided me with one special benefit. To this day, I am frequently greeted by former students that I encounter throughout the community. As my vision has faded in recent years, they usually have to identify themselves, but their memories have not faded. The things they remember have given me a wonderful retrospective of what we accomplished together and of times that were of special value and importance to them.

It was all a joy!

This Santa Was a She

As a teacher of young children, I came to think that their interest in Santa Claus and the excitement it generates might be useful in their lessons at Christmastime. It was clear that a visit from him could be a real motivator!

However, there were not many male teachers in the elementary schools when I was a young teacher, which meant that there was no one who would naturally step in to play the role of the jolly old elf. So, beginning in 1941 at the four-teacher Burlison School where I taught third and fourth grades, I took on the role myself.

I traveled to Memphis and bought my first Santa suit at Sears. With the permission of Ed Glover, my Principal, I transformed myself into Santa while my students were off to physical education class. Then I hid in a coat closet that was in a corner of the classroom. When the children returned to my room, the Principal was there to tell them that I had to leave for a few minutes and that he would stay with them for the Christmas party we were about to have.

After the children had settled in and while the Principal was speaking to them, Santa began to shake his jingle bells in the closet. This immediately got the attention of the children who looked toward the closet just as Santa stepped out and greeted them! Their delight far exceeded my expectations! The children's surprise and excitement was really something to see—especially in those dreary days of World War II.

Santa joined the class and the volunteer room-mothers who had come to help with the party and the gift exchange. After the party was well underway, Santa took leave of the children and left them with a promise that he would visit each of their homes on Christmas Eve night. Then he slipped out the door and went down the hall accompanied by a happy chorus of "Good-bye, Santa!"

A few minutes later, Miss Vivian, now playing the role of herself, came into the classroom and told the children that she had just bumped into Santa Claus down the hall! The children, of course, were eager to tell me all about the special visit I had missed.

My portrayal of Santa at Christmastime became one of my traditions for all of my thirty-five years of teaching. While the game changed with the older children, it was always a fun event. One time I was in the ladies room adjusting my beard when one of the second graders came in and saw me standing there in front of the mirror. Without missing a beat, she gently took my hand and led me to the door, explaining, "Santa, you are in the wrong bathroom." She led me over to the boys' lavatory and said, "This is where you should be, Santa. This is the one for boys." I went in as directed.

I really enjoyed playing Santa Claus, and I eventually decided that I did not have to restrict my performances to the school. For years on Christmas Eve, I would visit the homes of friends and neighbors who had little children.

Occasionally, the family would invite me in to say hello, but most times, I just tapped on the window of the room where the family was gathered, rang my jingle bells, waved to the children, bellowed a big "Ho! Ho! Ho!" then went on my way. The latter approach was especially effective for those pre-adolescents kids who had begun to doubt that there was a Santa—until they saw me tapping on the window.

From those home visits, I graduated to appearing as Santa in Brighton's Christmas parade. One year when I was riding on the Santa float, I was bothered by a bad cough. As luck would have it, the parade came to a temporary stop right in front of the Wells Grocery Store. One of the "helpers" who was on the float with me ran into Wells and bought me some cough drops that helped get me through the rest of the parade. A Christmas kindness!

I also appeared as Santa in many Christmas parades riding in my parents' restored 1949 Chevrolet. Daddy and Mother had bought the car new in 1949, and they and my brother Rudy drove it for many years. When it was retired, it was still in pretty good shape, so we brought it out to our property in Clopton and stored it out by the barn for many more years. In the late 1980s, I had it restored to its original condition, and she was a beauty! Santa rode in it in Christmas parades in Brighton, Covington, and Munford, oftentimes throwing candy to the children along the route.

Then came an unwelcome opportunity to play Santa in an unwanted venue. In the early-1990s, I found myself admitted to Methodist Hospital North in Memphis and recovering from a small stroke. I tried my best to convince my doctors that I was well enough to be released in time to have Christmas at home. I promised the doctors that, if they allowed me to go home for Christmas, I would come back to the hospital on the 26th; I did not prevail.

Finally, out of frustration, I told my primary doctor that if he did not allow me to go home for Christmas, I would run away and Santa Claus was going to take my place. Even such an ominous threat, delivered on Christmas Eve, did not work. I was captive in the hospital for Christmas.

As soon as the doctor left the room, I whimpered a little bit then directed Mary Nelle to go home and retrieve a large white box from the top drawer of a chest in the attic. While I did not tell her what was in it, she had her suspicions.

On her way back to the hospital, she stopped at a nearby Target store and purchased a small Christmas tree, a string of lights, and some tiny ornaments. When she got back to my room, she handed me the large white box, and while she decorated the room, I transformed myself into Santa Claus, beard and all. There I was, a grown woman, old enough to know better, lying in my hospital bed wearing two IVs and a heart monitor, *now dressed as Santa Claus!*

Shortly after Santa took my place, the door to my room opened and a young nurse's aide came into the room carrying a carafe of fresh ice water. She got about half way into the room before she looked my way. As soon as she saw Santa propped up in bed instead of the lady she expected, she froze in her tracks! Slowly, without turning her back on me, she started back-stepping toward the door.

As she got almost to the door, still carrying the ice water and staring at me, she asked "Are you the *real* Santa Claus?"

I responded, "Ho! Ho! Ho! Yes, I am!"

She quickly darted out the opened door and hurried down the hall to the nurses' station. Within seconds, she returned with a cluster of other nurses. They burst into my room, saw Santa lying there in the bed amid the pillows and tubes and monitors, and the peels of laughter began.

Word went out up and down the hall and to adjacent floors that Santa was there as a patient. That brought a steady stream of hospital staff, nurses, and doctors, including my own medical team, who came to greet Santa. Everyone had to pose for photos with Santa. My doctor's office still displays a photo with him hugging St. Nick!

What a party we all had! I'm not sure that this is what the doctor had in mind when he decided that I should stay in the hospital through the Christmas holiday, but we made the most of a difficult situation.

I was finally discharged that next week, and our family celebrated with all our usual traditions, which seemed even more meaningful that particular year. Being back together at home proved clearly for each of us that Christmas is much more that a specific day on the calendar—it is a season of the heart.

Dear Reader,

Mem's Santa gigs did not end with her 1991 performance as the old elf while hooked up to two IVs and a heart monitor when she was hospitalized for a small stroke. For years following that appearance, she visited the same hospital on Christmas afternoon. Dressed in full Santa gear, she stopped by each nurses' station to say "Ho! Ho! Ho!" and check in with her friends, old and new. Then she went from room to room delivering candy, small gifts, and, of course, hugs to patients, their families, and the staff. She became a holiday regular!

"Santa" and Mary Nelle celebrate Christmas
at Methodist Hospital North in Memphis while Vivian
was grounded as a patient over the holidays in 1991.

Splitting the Scene

A missing child is a serious, frightening problem for everybody, especially for those responsible for his care.

Once in the early 1970s, one of my sixth grade boys did not return to my room after physical education class, which was just before the end of the school day. Every afternoon, the physical education teacher would take my students for a thirty-minute class. While they were gone, I had a planning period. When they returned, there was only half an hour left before the final bell rang, and we settled down for some storytelling to end the day on a calm note.

Like most days, this one ended without incident—or so I thought—and I went home at the usual time. About 4:30, Mr. Bennett, the school Principal called. One of my students, Raymond Griffin, had not come home from school. His mother called the school to inquire about him. Mr. Bennett called me to see if I knew anything about him. I was able to confirm that he had been in school, but I suddenly realized that I had no recollection of seeing him those last few minutes at the end of the day. I quickly got in the car and headed back to school.

Shortly after I got there, members of the Sheriff's
Department arrived in response to Mr. Bennett's call for
help. School staff and the Sheriff's people began a
systematic search of the all the school buildings, including
some old ones that were adjacent. They went down toward
the creek and into the woods behind the school grounds, but
they found no trace of him. Other locals joined the search.
The longer he was missing, the more frightened we all
became.

While at the school, on Mr. Bennett's request, I called
Raymond's mother to see if she had heard from him yet.
Still nothing.

It was beginning to get dark, and there did not seem to be
anything else that I could do at the school so Mr. Bennett
told me to go home and wait. The Sheriff's deputies
continued to search until night fell, then they, too, went
home. We were all genuinely worried.

Later that evening, I got a call from Raymond's mother
saying that he had finally arrived at home and was O.K. She
apologized for having stirred up all of this trouble. She was
not able to talk further because she had other people to
notify.

The next morning, I found out from Mr. Bennett what had
happened...

During PE class, Raymond split the seam in the seat of his
pants. He was very embarrassed and felt that he could not
return to class in that condition. He also felt that he could

not walk through town with his underpants hanging out. What was he to do to avoid all of the embarrassment and the teasing by his fellow sixth-graders?

Think about it. What would any of us do?

With the seat of his pants torn out, Raymond made a plan... He decided to hide in the woods until darkness fell. Not a bad solution, but he did not figure that so many people would miss him. After it was dark, he made his way home without running into any of his classmates or other townsfolk. Of course, the next day, everyone knew the true story!

Raymond was a reluctant celebrity and the "butt" of a lot of jokes. His escapade was also the cause of the entire school getting a lecture from Mr. Bennett on the problems of not showing up where and when you are expected.

From that day forward, I stationed myself at my classroom door and counted every head when the children returned from PE class or any other activity that took them from my care for even a brief portion of the day.

And Raymond gave a whole new meaning to the phrases, "spitting the scene" and doing something "by the seat of your pants"!

Dear Reader,

Years later, my mother had her own episode of "splitting the scene" at Brighton School. She had a lovely black eyelet dress that she usually wore only to church or on dressy occasions. Uncharacteristically, she wore it to school one day.

I was in college at the time and was still at home for the summer. Out of the blue, she called from school and directed me to her closet. She told me to bring her a certain dress and to do it immediately.

Of course, I asked why. I remember her response was something like: "Just do it NOW!" I obeyed.

As it turns out, she was playing baseball with some students and was at bat when the split happened. She swung at a pitch and hit the ball with all her might. In doing so, the force of her swing popped the thin portions of fabric between the pretty cut-out patterns in the eyelet fabric and split open the entire back of her nice dress!

Unlike Raymond, she did not have the luxury of hiding in the woods!

~~~MNMcL

The Beaning

All twelve years that my daughter Mary Nelle was a student at Brighton School, we went to great pains to make sure that she was never in my class. We rode to school together each day and saw a lot of each other in special situations at school, but I did everything I could to make sure that our home lives and our school lives did not intersect. One day, however, they did, and they did so without warning.

It happened when Mary Nelle was a junior in high school and her classes were in the "big building" that was just across the driveway from the classroom where I was teaching sixth grade. As she was walked out of the building on this particular day, she casually noticed a crowd of kids that had gathered in a clump farther out on the elementary playground. They were all abuzz and trying to see what was going on in the center of a circle of kids. It appeared to her like those scenes when students would get into a fight at recess and a crowd would gather to watch the action and egg on the combatants.

She paid little attention to the commotion and continued on her way until someone called to her, yelling: *"Mary Nelle! It's your mother!"*

Her first thought was *"My mother's in a fight?"*

With that, she headed reluctantly toward the crowd. When she arrived at the cluster of onlookers that were staring down into the circle, she wiggled her way to the front and discovered that the attraction really was me—all stretched out on the ground, knocked out cold!

The kids who were standing around were quick to tell her that I had been hit in the head with a baseball during recess and that I had fallen from the chair on which I had been sitting to supervise the children at recess. The high school baseball team was practicing on the ball field nearby and one of the players hit a foul ball that flew over the protective fence around the playground and drove its way straight to my noggin.

All I remember was the most awful sounding thud. It sounded like someone had hit a drum. As I came to, everything was swirling, and I felt like I was under water. My vision was blurry. The leaves on the trees seemed to be fuzzy and moving, as if they were all submerged.

Mr. Bennett, the Principal of all twelve grades, was already on the scene, and he assured Mary Nelle that I would be O.K. He had called the doctor and was advised that I would probably be all right, but I should not be allowed to fall asleep.

After recess, my students and I returned to our classroom. For the rest of the day, the children were so quiet and respectful that it was hard *not* to fall asleep.

The ballplayer who hit the errant ball that struck me came over to apologize. To my surprise—and his—he turned out to be the guy that Mary Nelle was dating at the time!

Not only did Phillip Dickey have to face up to the impact of his foul ball on a teacher that day, but I had plenty of opportunities to jokingly remind him of it each time he came to pick up Mary Nelle for a date and even for their prom.

Pek Gunn Poetry

One day a few years ago, while I was walking through the Covington Walmart, a grown man came up behind me, and, without identifying himself, quietly began reciting in my ear:

> In Nashville, every family boasts
> Of five rooms and a bath.
> But in my youth, I never had
> But three rooms and a path.

I immediately started laughing and turned around to greet one of my former sixth graders who was remembering a portion of a poem that I taught to my children every year.

Standing in the middle of a shopping aisle, he had recited the opening stanza of "Three Rooms and a Path," an enjoyable poem by Pek Gunn, the Tennessee Poet Laureate whom I was honored to know as a personal acquaintance.

All of Pek Gunn's work was perfect for grabbing the attention of young adolescents and engaging them in the fun of words and language and poetry. His poems were such fun to read out loud, and I used them often with my classes. Our favorite of his books was *Tumbln' Creek Tales*[1] which contained the quoted poem. Almost all of the children enjoyed listening to them, and little by little many of my students memorized his poems, especially this particular one.

Over the years, as I have run into my former sixth-grade pupils, the "Three Rooms and a Path" poem was a shared motto or code that connected us. Very often it was mentioned as one of the most fun and lasting things that "my children" remembered from being in my class.

For years after I retired, I spent Fridays working at a charity shop called the"The Hub." This is an outreach project of Clopton United Methodist Church established in the former TR Gray and Sons Store right there in our rural community. The Hub accepts donations of used goods and sells them to people who have a need for or an interest in such things. My days at The Hub provided many opportunities for me to encounter former students as well as their parents or their children or both. It helped keep me connected to this community and its people for over twenty-five years since my retirement.

One afternoon while working at The Hub, I became aware of a gathering of four young ladies who had come in separately, but now clustered over on the north side of the building behind the racks of ladies clothing. I was aware of buzzing and giggling coming from their direction, but I decided to remain behind the counter minding my own business. Shortly, the four ladies approached the counter as a group. This was a bit strange, but, because of my vision loss to Macular Degeneration, I still had no idea who they were or what was in the works.

When the four reached the counter, they introduced themselves, and I immediately recognized them all as former students of mine! We had a nice visit, and I asked them about their families and where they were living now and what their lives were like. They were kind enough to inquire about my health and my life as a retired teacher. After we chatted for a while, they awkwardly let me know that they had something they wanted to give me.

After a few false starts and a lot more giggles, they began in unison to recite one of the Pek Gunn's poems I used to read them:

> In Nashville, every family boasts
> Of five rooms and a bath.
> But in my youth I never had
> But three rooms and a path.
>
> They built the outhouse on the brink
> Of Tumblin Creek, and then
> Each time I passed I had an urge
> To push the outhouse in.
>
> For weeks I fought that powerful urge,
> And one day I was weak
> I slipped out to the outhouse and
> I pushed it in the creek

That night my Dad called me aside
And all he had to say
Was "Do you know who pushed the house
Into the creek today?"

I told my Dad that it was I
He didn't even chide
But then and there with a leather belt
Prepared to tan my hide.

"But Daddy," I said, George Washington
Cut down the cherry tree
He told the truth and so his Pa
Let little George go free."

"But let me ask you something, son"
My Dad said with a frown,
"Was his Pa in the cherry tree
When Georgie cut it down?"

These ladies were so proud that together they had remembered all the words to that favorite old poem. Once again and years later, poetry was a bond that tied us together.

[1]Richard McKeel "Pek" Gunn, *Tumblin' Creek Tales*, (Nashville: Tumblin' Creek Enterprises, ©1963.)

Miss Vivian, a Real Rock Star

Having taught children in the Brighton area for thirty-five years, I am blessed to frequently run into former students at stores, in church, at restaurants, and everywhere I go. My son-in-law Rick even said, "Memmie, you're always running into someone you know, giving hugs, and kissing babies. Being with you is like being with a politician!"

As my vision has become poor in my old age, I feel especially grateful when these former students come up and identify themselves in these unexpected places. We usually laugh and share good stories of our work together in school, and some have been nice enough to give me credit for some good things that happened to them as a result of something they learned in my classroom.

In 2007, the spring of my ninetieth year, I was sitting on the patio at my home on McLennan Road when a young man stopped by to say hello. As often happens with these mini-reunions, we reminisced about his time in school and in my class. He looked at the variety of rocks that filled the many shelves that line the patio and said, "Every time I think of you as a teacher, I remember how much I learned from our study of rocks." His comment set me to thinking about how this interest in geology came to be so important in my life.

In 1903, the Illinois Central Railroad decided to extend its north-south line through west Tennessee. While much of our region's countryside is flat farmland, there are a number of beautiful rolling hills close to the Mississippi River. Rather than have its tracks follow the ups and downs of this undulating countryside, the railroad decided to create a bed as level as possible for their trains to travel when heading into and out of Memphis.

The town of Brighton was built on a very low-lying, level plain while the town of Atoka, just six miles to the south, was located on higher ground. To create a level path for the train, the Illinois Central Railroad decided to move around some dirt in west Tennessee. They dug a deep cut through the hills of Atoka and built bridges to carry the roads of Atoka across this man-made chasm.

The dirt that came from the Atoka cut was hauled to Brighton and used to create an elevated railroad bed in the west section of town. The bed was about thirty feet above the low plain of the town, and two concrete archways were built through the embankment to permit our east-west streets to pass under the railroad. This elevated railroad bed and our narrow archways have been identifiable landmarks in Brighton for over 100 years.

For all of my life, I have wondered how they cut that gorge
in Atoka and hauled all of that dirt to Brighton. How many
men and animals were involved in this project? Who decided
where to dig and where to dump? How could one decision
by railroad company executives in Chicago create so many
changes in two small towns so many miles away?

Frequently, on Sunday afternoons when I was a child,
Mother would take Rudy, Nelle, and me for long walks along
the railroad bed. We would pick up rocks and toss them. We
would always be on the lookout for items that may have
fallen from a train.

Mother would always be the first to hear the approach of a
distant train. If the train was coming from the south, we
would move to the other side of the southbound track. If it
was coming from the north, we would move to the opposite
side. As the train got closer, Mother would gather us all in a
huddle with her arms around the three of us, and we would
all hug each other until the train passed.

As a young one, I sometimes wondered what we would do if
two trains came at the same time from opposite directions? I
guess there was enough room on the berm on either side of
the tracks that we would have been safe while the trains
passed, but this never happened during our many Sunday
afternoon walks.

The real fascination of these walks for me was the rocks.
There were rocks of all shapes, colors, and sizes along the
railroad bed. There were different kinds of rocks composed
of different minerals. Rudy and I would pick up the ones

that really appealed to us and carry them home. One Sunday Mother presented us with bags for our rocks. She had made them from green material that she had brought home from the store. The bags even had handles. Rudy's bag was larger than mine because he could carry more rocks. But I came home from every railroad walk with my green bag filled with rocks to add to my collection.

My rock collection grew and lived in Daddy's garage until I became a teacher. In going through a science unit on geology and rock formations one year, I suddenly realized that I might be able to use my collection to make this unit come alive for my students. Perhaps I could get them to be as interested in rocks as I have been!

I came to realize that the students were also fascinated by the rocks, so my husband Bill built a cabinet ten feet long for my classroom at Brighton School. The cabinet had three shelves that allowed me to display the rocks, clearly identified and neatly arranged. I used cord to attach three books about rocks to the cabinet; one dangled at each end and one hung in the middle. During times when students had finished their lessons and had study time to spend while others were finishing assignments, I permitted and encouraged them to go to the rock collection to read about the rocks and study those that were available to them.

As this study of rocks grew in size and popularity, a wonderful resource appeared and made it even better. One Sunday while attending our Clopton United Methodist Church, I helped welcome a new couple that had moved to our community from Memphis. Charlie and Emily

McPherson brought with them their own strong interest in
rocks and a marvelous collection that far exceeded what was
available even in most museums in the area. Quickly, the
McPhersons became my allies, and before long I was
organizing an annual field trip of my students to their home
to explore their collection. In anticipation of our visit, the
McPhersons would arrange an egg carton for each child with
a different specimen of rock in each compartment. During
our visit, the students were challenged to identify the rocks in
their cartons. When they did, I typed the rock's name on a
small piece of paper, and the student glued it to the carton in
the proper location—sorta like the way they label candy in a
Whitman's Sampler! At the end of the trip, each child took
home an egg carton with its rocks as the beginning of his or
her own little collection.

I didn't realize that I had gained a reputation as the "rock-
teacher," but eventually learned how far that reputation had
spread. One day a Tipton County road crew was digging
near Richardson's Landing down by the Mississippi River
when they heard a loud thud. They dug further and
unearthed a large petrified stump. A discussion ensued about
what they should do with this unusual find. Later that day,
they delivered that petrified stump to the Baird Hardware
Store with a note attached saying that the stump was to be
given to "Miss Vivian." I guess I had arrived. I was now a
"rock star"!

It wasn't long before the huge stump joined the rock
collection in my classroom. I told the story of the mysterious
appearance of the petrified log to my class every year, and
soon it became a favorite attraction of many students.

One of the advantages of having my classroom in the northeast corner of Brighton School was that I could park my car just outside the building and have a short walk to my room. One morning just as I was getting out of my car, I heard a dreadful thud coming from the direction of my room. A "thud" means trouble in any case, so I took off running.

As I entered the room, some students were standing in a circle in the middle of the room, looking down at the floor. They were staring at the petrified stump—or at least part of it. Then I saw another hunk of the stump on the floor nearby. Someone had broken my precious stump! In the middle of the circle stood Leland, the largest, strongest sixth-grader I had ever taught.

I immediately sent for Mr. Bennett, the Principal. He arrived quickly as I was asking Leland, "What was that noise I heard?"

Leland explained, "I was trying to see how many times I could pump the stump. I got it up in the air one time and it fell!"

Well, you can imagine what I wanted to do to Leland, despite the fact that he was the largest sixth-grader I had ever had! Instead, Mr. Bennett took Leland to the office and had him spend two hours sitting there thinking about what he had done.

I still have the pieces of my petrified stump, but I never remember that story without regretting that Leland, as a young man, was killed in a gun fight in South Carolina.

Suddenly I heard a male voice saying, "Miss Vivian? …Miss Vivian?"

It was my former student who had stopped by, still sitting there on the patio with me. I had let my mind wander, reflecting on how much these rocks have formed a solid foundation for so much of my teaching—and so much of my life.

Then we continued our visit.

Mary Nelle—Some Things Don't Change

Bill and I were married in 1941, and we looked forward to having a child of our own. Our hope was to have four children in all. When we did not get pregnant after the first two years, we consulted a specialist in Memphis for his advice. He provided us samples of a drug that was supposed to help couples conceive, and we went home with our little red pills and hoped for the best. Within a few months, we realized that the pills, or something, had worked and our first child was on her way.

In December, 1944, our little girl was born. It had been a difficult pregnancy and a dangerous birth, but when I looked at her, I knew that all the pain and suffering were well worth it. By previous agreement, Bill and I had decided that if the baby were a boy, I would get to choose his name. But if the baby were a girl, Bill would have the honors. He decided that, if we had a girl, she would be named for both my sister Nelle and me. My formal name was "Mary Vivian," but I never liked the name Mary and preferred just "Vivian." When the time came to name our little girl, Bill combined "Mary" in honor of me and "Nelle" in honor of my sister.

From the beginning, Bill always used both names when referring to our daughter. She came to be known as "Mary Nelle," a beautiful but unusual combination that is not heard very often. Of course, this double name led to a lifetime of our daughter correcting people who want to call her simply "Mary." She usually tells people, "It's Mary Nelle—like Billy Bob." Now that she's living in Pennsylvania, above the Mason Dixon line, she's jokingly known as "Never-Just-Mary"!

As Mary Nelle was growing up, it was apparent early on that she was a strong-willed person. One morning when she was still in a high chair, I remarked that the grapefruit that I was eating that morning was particularly sour. Because she had the other half of this same grapefruit, I suggested that she not eat it because it would not taste good. She insisted that it would be O.K. and took a taste. She grimaced, and I said "You don't have to eat that, honey, its' not good." Through clinched teeth, she defiantly declared, "Tis good, Memmie!" and took another taste. Again, I said, "Mary Nelle, it's not good." Again, she firmly insisted "Tis good, Memmie!" Then she stubbornly continued with each bite, followed by a big grimace, until her half of the grapefruit was gone.

Early on, I suspected that Mary Nelle had trouble seeing. When we went to the movie together and sat near the back, she would complain that she could not see the screen, and we noticed that she missed some of the action and details of the shows. She preferred to sit up front, and this began to worry me. One afternoon, we attended the Disney movie "Cinderella" with Mary Nelle and some of her cousins. On our way home, the children were discussing the scene in which the mice were making a necklace for Cinderella by threading pearls on their tails. Mary Nelle did not remember that scene and insisted that it had not been in the movie she saw. This happened several times as the children discussed the movie, and I was shocked by how much she was missing.

Just to be sure my observation was accurate, the next day Mary Nelle and I returned to see Cinderella by ourselves. Knowing what was coming, I let her choose the row where we would sit, and she took us all the way to the very front of the theater. This confirmed what I feared.

In the next few days, we got in to see a Memphis eye doctor that our family had used for several years. He examined her eyes and confirmed that she would need glasses. Mary Nelle, overhearing the conversation, was frightened and quietly began to cry because she did not want to wear glasses. The doctor recommended that we have the lenses placed in plain wire-rimmed frames and sent us off to the optician. As we were leaving the office and stepped into the hall, my sister, Nelle, attempting to help Mary Nelle feel better about what we had just learned, suggested that we would buy her very pretty plastic frames that she would enjoy wearing. Somehow, the doctor overheard Nelle's comment and followed us out into the hall. In no uncertain terms, he let us know that he did not want her to have glasses with plastic frames. Plain wire-rims were his only option. Of course, between the time we left the ophthalmologist's office and reached the optician, we had decided for ourselves that fun glasses would be best for this little five-year old. A cousin who was working for the optician agreed that the wire-rimmed glasses would not be any more effective than the fancy ones, so we went home with very pretty blue and pink plastic frames, which were the first of many styles to come.

When we got home, we were eager to try out the new glasses and see what difference they made. I called Mary Nelle over to the front window of our living room and asked her to look out on the field across the road from our house. I asked her what she saw. She replied, "I see the field across the road, Memmie." Then I asked her to put on her new glasses and again asked her what she saw. She did and she said, "I see a cow in the field now. She just ran up there."

She pulled off the glasses again as I asked her to, and she said, "The cow just ran away, Memmie! She's gone!" When she put the glasses back on, she exclaimed, "Look, Memmie! The cow just ran back up there!" Each time she took the glasses off, the cow was gone. We had fun with this little exercise, but it took us a while to convince her that the cow was not coming and going, but rather she was able to see things with her glasses that she could not see without them. Stubborn again…

Throughout her childhood, Mary Nelle had to return to the ophthalmologist every six months for a check-up. This continued from the time she was six until she was sixteen. Every six months the doctor changed her prescription because her vision continued to worsen. It was difficult for her vision to get adjusted to each new lens prescription every six months. Just as she was growing accustomed to the added correction strength, it was time to change again. This became quite a story in our family, and we were all looking forward to her vision stabilizing.

One day her Daddy said to her, "The first time you go to the eye doctor and he does not have to change your glasses, we will celebrate by buying you whatever you want." Sure enough, in her sixteenth year, Mary Nelle went to the eye doctor, and, for the first time since she was five, he did not need to change the strength of her glasses! She could not wait to get home to tell her Daddy!

Bill was a man of his word and told her that she could choose whatever she wanted as a reward for reaching this great milestone. She remembered that we had talked about someday buying her a new bedroom suite, and that's what she told him she wanted. Bill swallowed hard at that and suggested that we begin shopping for one the next day. After several shopping trips and thoroughly searching the major furniture departments in Memphis, she chose a three-piece solid cherry set with a lovely four-poster bed in a spool pattern. That suite is in her home today.

Mary Nelle also had trouble with her Eustachian tubes, which caused her many ear problems all during her life. On one visit with a very prominent Ear, Nose, and Throat specialist in Memphis when she was still very young, she again proved her stubborn streak. The doctor was performing a procedure to change the air pressure in her ear channels. He was trying to get her to speak as part of the treatment, but each time she did, it caused a terribly sharp pain throughout all her sinuses.

That did it! The battle was on. The doctor was trying to get her to speak, and she was determined to remain silent to avoid the pain. Finally, looking at a large wall poster that featured a little girl holding a cute kitten, the doctor said to her, "Call the kitty, Mary Nelle. Call the kitty."

I nearly fell off my chair when young Mary Nelle screwed up her face and demanded of the doctor, "*If you want the cat, you call him yourself.*"

A real turning point in Mary Nelle's ability to stand on her own two feet came in the summer after the fourth grade. She came home from school one day and announced that she would not be going to the 4-H Club Camp as planned. In his very understanding manner, Bill asked her why the change in plans. She replied, "None of my friends will be going. Kay and Betty and Carol Ann told me that they weren't going. So now I can't go because I won't have any friends there."

As usual, Bill listened patiently. Then he firmly assured her, "You can still go. You don't have to do only what your friends do. This'll be an opportunity for you to make new friends. You will be fine."

When the time to go to camp grew near, I could tell that, while Mary Nelle always believed that her Daddy would never steer her wrong, she was not sure that he was right this time. As the day approached to go to the Court House in Covington to meet the bus, I could see that she was hanging back and reluctant to go away for a week without her usual friends. During our drive to Covington, I reminded her of what her Daddy had said and that we believed in her and that everything would work out well.

After we arrived at the Court House and parked the car, she tucked her pillow under her arm and approached the bus that would transport them to camp at UT Martin. Suddenly, I was amazed at how she waded into this group of kids, none of whom she had ever met before. There she was, shaking hands and asking names and introducing herself to all her fellow campers-to-be! By the time the children got on the bus, she was in the midst of a happy buzz. She took a seat by a window and waved to me as the bus pulled away. Of course I was concerned for her, but confident that everything would be all right.

One week later, I found myself back at the Court House waiting for the bus to return the campers. The calls from Mary Nelle during the week had been reassuring, but, even with that, I was not really prepared for the happy and connected group of kids who got off that bus. Right in the middle of the laughing and hugging campers was Mary Nelle who, only a week before, had worried about having no friends in the group of campers. Here she was, returning with so many new friends that she didn't want to break away to go home!

She's still stubborn and friendly.

Some things just don't change.

Winfield Brown McLennan

The Cornelius (Neil) and Flora McLennan family first arrived in west Tennessee in the 1830s. Neil had been born in Loch Carron, Scotland, in 1787 and immigrated to North Carolina. Flora Murchison McLennan was born in 1809 into a Scottish family that lived in Moore County, North Carolina. In the countryside of Tipton County Tennessee, about forty miles north of the young city of Memphis, these hard-working Scots were responsible for the development of a small community in what is now the western edge of Clopton. Their farm extended over hundreds of acres, and their settlement grew to include their own general store, sawmill, gristmill, and cotton gin. McLennan families have lived on and worked that rich area of Tipton County for more than 175 years.

Neil and Flora had eleven children and lived in a large log house on the south side of the current McLennan Road, near the busy enterprises they built. As their children and grandchildren grew up, most of them built their homes along a road that ran through their community. Around 1970, that route was formally named McLennan Road, confirming the common usage of local people who had called it McLennan Road for more than 100 years.

Sometime before 1885, Neil and Flora's son Daniel, known as "Dock," built a home on the north side of the road, across from the community businesses. There he and his wife Emma Adkins reared their family of three daughters and four sons. One of those boys was Daniel McLennan Jr. who was born in that house in 1885.

As a young man, Dan Jr. was a streetcar motorman in Memphis until he decided to return to the family farm in Clopton. In 1911, he married Bertie Ophelia Poindexter, the daughter of Virginia Clifton and Christopher Columbus Poindexter, another prominent and respected family in southern Tipton County. One of thirteen children, Bertie attended MCFI—the Memphis Conference Female Institute —in Jackson, Tennessee. Before marrying Dan, she was a teacher.

After returning to Tipton County and establishing his own family, "Mr. Dan"—as everyone referred to Dan Jr. in his adult and senior years—continued to work the family farmland. On the property they named "Lone Oak Farm," he established a thriving business growing and shipping sweet potatoes. He also involved himself in politics and held prominent positions in the Democratic party for many years. He was part of the grass-roots movement to establish what became the Southwest Tennessee Electric Membership Corporation; those efforts helped bring electricity to rural west Tennessee.

During those same years, Miss Bertie ran the family home, was a pillar of Clopton Methodist Church, hosted the family for a large Thanksgiving-like dinner *every* Sunday after church, and cooked a full noonday meal for all the farmworkers five days a week! She was a tiny, efficient lady with a quick wit and generous soul.

By 1917, Mr. Dan and Miss Bertie, with their four-year-old son Malcolm, were living in the tall house where Mr. Dan had been born. It was a large, two-story, white frame farmhouse that sat back a distance from McLennan Road. It had a deep porch that ran along its entire front, and it often served as the meeting place for this branch of the McLennan family, especially on hot summer Sunday afternoons.

On July 14, 1917, thirty-two-year-old Dan set down a basket of peaches on the bench next to the kitchen door and declared, "I do believe today is the hottest day of the year." Then he explained to Bertie, "These peaches are ready for canning, but by tomorrow they will be too soft."

The twenty-seven-year-old Bertie took this in stride because she had heard it all before. In the meantime, she was juggling two projects that day as well as caring for four-year-old Malcolm. She was doing the weekly ironing of the clothes she had washed the previous day. She was also tending to another batch of peaches that she was cooking in preparation for canning. Dan had built a fire in the kitchen range to furnish heat for the smoothing irons and for cooking the peaches at the same time.

Bertie would pause to stir the peaches, and then return to her ironing. She quietly took pleasure in the smell of the cooking peaches and in the look and feel of the freshly ironed clothes. Bertie was a consummate homemaker and farm wife, and she prided herself on all that she accomplished for her family.

By mid-afternoon, the peach preserves on the stove were ready to can. About that time, Bertie took off her apron and announced that someone else would have to finish both the canning and the ironing. The labor pains that she was experiencing were telling her that she had another priority. Dan summoned the local physician, Dr. Brown, as Bertie's labor pains continued.

Ada, Dan's sister, and her husband Charlie Miller came to help complete the chores. Dan's brother Jim and his wife Lizzie also came over for a "visit." Both couples lived on McLennan Road, just east of Dan and Bertie's home.

Just before midnight, their second son was born, and they named him Winfield Brown McLennan. "Winfield" was a family name from Scotland. "Brown" was chosen in honor of Dr. Brown, the family physician and close personal friend who delivered the baby.

Dr. Brown, who lived nearby on what is now Sawmill Road, spent the night with the family. After a breakfast of ham and eggs, he got on his horse and headed for home. He returned the next day to check on Bertie and Winfield and determined that they were both doing well. He also observed that, with the name of Brown, the baby was sure to turn out to be a very nice person.

Winfield grew up as part of the large McLennan family on the farm in Clopton, and it was there that he acquired his nickname. As a very young child, he constantly trailed behind one of his father's farmhands. Everywhere Bill Morrison went, Winfield followed him. Bill Morrison would tie Winfield's red wagon to the back of the farm cart that he was taking out into the fields. Winfield would go along for the ride then stay with him in the field. The other farmhands said that everywhere they saw Bill Morrison, they would see "little Bill." The name stuck, and Winfield fondly became "Bill" to everyone—everyone, that is, except his mother!

Bill attended the Clopton School for his lower grades. After the eighth grade there, he and other Clopton students went to high school in Brighton. I first met him when we were freshman classmates there at Brighton High School.

Bill and I were both interested in school sports, and we began sitting together at the basketball games during our freshman year when, because of injuries, we were both unable to play for our respective basketball teams. In December of our freshman year, Bill had shot himself in the foot (literally!) in a life-threatening hunting accident, so he was unable to play that season. Earlier that same year, I had broken my ankle while climbing over a pile of logs that had been dumped in our neighborhood by an overturned logging truck. This prevented me from playing basketball, but it provided Bill and me with opportunities to sit together during the games we were sitting out.

In addition to being with him at the games, I figured out when he had his regular follow-up appointments with Dr. Billy McLister for his foot injury. Conveniently for me, Dr. Billy's office was near my Daddy's store so I would *just happen* to show up at the doctor's office. Then, while Bill was seeing the doctor, I visited with his mother.

As Bill and I became more of "an item" around the school, our English teacher, Fentress Huffman, was the first to comment on the fact that we were both called "Bill." He said, "Well, I guess two 'Bills' belong together."

Later that year, when Bill started driving to the basketball games, he began to offer me a ride home after the game. Soon he started to pick me up at my home before the game and give me a ride in both directions.

During our high school years, Bill and I became close friends and saw a lot of each other. Our relationship resulted in my deciding to attend the State Teachers College in Memphis rather than follow my brother and sister to Bryson College 250 miles away in Fayetteville, near Nashville. When I took my first teaching job in Burlison, Bill was my constant companion, and he used his carpentry skills to help me improve my classroom.

On Saturday, January 11, 1941, I remember helping my mother cook the midday dinner. It was about 11 o'clock in the morning when I looked out the window and saw Bill McLennan coming up the driveway of the Baird home in Brighton. I was surprised that he was visiting so early in the day, but when he showed up, Mother invited him to stay and have dinner with us. Afterward, he invited me to ride with him to Atoka.

Once we got in his truck, I asked him, "Why are you going to Atoka?"

Bill replied "I ordered a ring for you from Mr. Fite, the jeweler, but it's not the right one so I want to return it."

I was not completely surprised since we had talked of marriage, and I expected to receive a ring eventually—but I was surprised that it was today! Then I said, "Let me see the ring." I was thrilled and excited, and I thought the ring was beautiful.

Curious about why he was returning it, I asked, "What's wrong with it?"

Bill explained that he had paid Mr. Fite a certain amount of money for a ring with a larger-sized diamond as described in the catalog. However, due to a recent increase in their prices, the company had sent a smaller diamond that matched the amount of the payment. Bill wanted to talk to Mr. Fite to see what could be done to replace it with the larger diamond he'd chosen.

I then opened my mouth. "Lets just keep this one!"

We did, and I still have that ring today, sixty-six years later, and am wearing it as I write this in 2007.

Bill and I set our wedding date for October 9, 1941. This worked well for me because it fell during cotton-picking season, and the schools were closed for six weeks during time for harvesting the cotton crops. As a teacher, I had a forced vacation during those weeks, so we decided that it would be a good time for a wedding and a honeymoon.

Earlier, on January 2 of 1941, Bill's father, Mr. Dan, sold him forty-five acres of the original McLennan land. This part of the farm had belonged to Bill's Aunt Ada, and it included the house where she and her family had lived. Over the next ten months, Bill worked tirelessly to refresh the old farmhouse and prepare it for us to live in after we were married. I helped when I was not teaching, and that became our own "home place."

As October neared, Daddy was feeling better, but was not yet able to move about. He was especially concerned that he would not be able to get up the very steep front steps of Brighton Presbyterian Church where the wedding was to be held. The more he worried, the more I worried. I could not imagine having a wedding without my daddy there to give me away. As Bill and I talked about it, we decided that perhaps we could get married at my home. We talked to Mother, Daddy, and the preacher, and no one had a reason why that would not work. We changed our plans and began to focus on having our wedding in the living room of the Baird home. Interestingly, this was the same room in which I had been born.

The day before the wedding, all of the wedding party and the Rev. Knox assembled at the Baird home for a rehearsal in the late afternoon. We were all there by the scheduled time except for one person...the groom! Bill had not arrived!

Where was Bill??? As you can imagine, I was the subject of a lot of good-natured teasing as time passed and Bill did not show up. The more time passed, the more nervous I became. Finally, I heard a loud roar coming up the hill from the direction of Daddy's store.

"There he comes now!" I said, relieved.

Jack Huffman quipped, "By the sound of it, he must be flying a plane."

Bill was flying, alright...flying in his truck! He had worked the overnight shift at the Dupont ammunition plant in Millington. Instead of going straight home and getting some sleep as was his usual custom after working the "graveyard" shift, he had some work to finish at the house that we would be moving into after the honeymoon. It was about noon that day before he laid down to get some sleep. When he woke up and saw that he had overslept and was late for the rehearsal, he moved quickly to get ready. He then hopped in his truck and raced to Brighton. Later, after the rehearsal, he asked his mother why she did not wake him so that he could make the rehearsal on time. With her eyes sparkling, Bertie said, "I figured you would wake up on your own since it was your wedding. I was sure you were interested enough to get there without my help!"

The wedding was scheduled for 6:00 P.M. on a Thursday. Mother had the house looking great, and my friend Verna

Gwinn played the piano as the guests arrived. Earlier in the day, the florist delivered two large baskets of flowers and two candelabra to place on either side of the location for the ceremony. We had chosen the window that faced east as the focal point of the ceremony. The flowers and candelabra were placed in front of the window and its full length draperies. Because the living room had a large thick rug with padding underneath, the flowers and candles were not as stable as they would have been on a hard surface. They wobbled a little each time someone passed by, but the florist felt that they would be secure for the short service.

My ten-year-old niece, Annette McCain, who for years had accompanied us on countless dates, was our soloist and sang "I Love You Truly." After the ceremony, she was miffed that we didn't take her along on our honeymoon!

As Bill and I greeted each other in front of the minister, the house was filled with family and friends. I'm sure it was a wonderful moment, but I was distracted. As Rev. Knox began the ceremony and proceeded with the prayers and his words of wisdom, I was transfixed by his gentle rocking from front to back. Each time he rocked backward, one of the unstable candelabras also rocked. I became totally preoccupied with the imminent possibility that Rev. Knox's rocking was going to cause the lighted candelabra to fall into the full-length drapes, which I was certain would cause an instant fire that would destroy my parents' house and threaten all of my friends…on my wedding day!

Somehow, we managed to get through the ceremony without a disaster. My friends told me how beautiful the ceremony was, but I was so worried about the candles that I missed most of it. Soon after the ceremony, Bill and I made our way to his car and sped off to our honeymoon. Our guests stayed for a wonderful party hosted by my parents.

Bill and I drove to Jackson, Tennessee, where we spent our wedding night. We then traveled across the state to Nashville and then to Gatlinburg before reaching our ultimate destination in North Carolina.

Nine days later we returned to Clopton where Bill's parents had assembled many of our family and friends, all of our new neighbors along McLennan Road, and many folks from the Clopton Methodist Church, which was to be an important part of our lives together. We had a most memorable and joyous "weenie roast" complete with a huge bonfire. It was a perfect completion of our wedding celebration!

Bill was a man of many talents. He had learned carpentry and engineering skills from his father, Mr. Dan, and he had a reputation as a very efficient builder. The men who knew his work often said that when he was done building a house, there was not enough scrap lumber left to fill a wheelbarrow.

In 1953, he used his skills to design and build us a four-bedroom brick home on that same knoll where our first home had rested. In fact, with the help of Basil Taylor and a crew of sturdy men, they actually moved the original house across the road, down the hill to the west, and up a rise to a new site. The moving process took about a week during the summer. We continued to live in the original house even as it was being moved and until the new home was complete! We moved into our new house just before Christmas that year, and it has remained my home ever since.

Bill's primary occupations were building houses and running the two concrete plants that he owned along with his brother, Malcolm. In addition, he farmed the McLennan land that had originally belonged to his Aunt Ada McLennan Miller, raising annual crops of cotton, soy beans, and corn. The rest of his acreage he used for his small herd of dairy cows. One of the biggest mistakes I made in my life was learning how to milk a cow! Every morning at 4 A.M., I was out in the dairy barn with Bill attaching the electric milkers, washing and steaming the buckets, working up a good appetite before breakfast *then* getting ready to go to school to teach the children. It was hard work, but we did it together.

Over the years, we added to our acreage by purchasing his Uncle Harry Poindexter's farm and other property that was adjacent to our original land. Also, at Mr. Dan's death in 1981, Bill inherited half of his father's portion of the original McLennan land that had come down through the generations.

Bill lived a generous life. He spent a lot of time using his skills to assist other people. He was always being called on to help someone unfreeze their pipes, or fix a problem with their electricity, or make a plumbing repair. He could never pass a stranded motorist without stopping to see if he could help. For many years during the 1970s and 1980s, he voluntarily maintained the Clopton Cemetery grounds and worked to restore the tombstones of community founders.

Bill and his cousin James McLennan gave many hours of
talented labor in support of Clopton United Methodist
Church. After the picturesque Clopton Church, built in
1910, was destroyed by fire in 1947, the congregation
purchased the chapel on the abandoned air base in Halls,
Tennessee. Bill and James, two strong young men in their
early thirties, worked on the crew that labeled and moved it
piece-by-piece to our church site then reassembled it in its
current location. Once they and the crew reconstructed it,
Bill and James poured a concrete floor for the entire large
basement. It was a huge task for just two men! For two days
running and without stopping to sleep, they mixed concrete,
poured it, and smoothed it by hand, working straight
through the night. James' wife Dorris Lee and I took them
food and hot coffee as they worked nonstop until the floor
was finished, almost forty-eight hours after they began. Years
later, Bill still felt badly about the single crack that developed
in that floor.

In addition to his many skills and talents, Bill was regarded
most highly for his kind, friendly, and humorous manner of
dealing with people. He loved to kid folks and crafted an
affectionate nickname for most of them. You could always
tell when he was up to something by his impish grin. He was
a friend to many and warmly respected by all who knew
him.

His people talents made him an especially good father for
our daughter Mary Nelle. He always made time for her, no
matter how busy he was. When she was sick, he cuddled her
and cradled her in his lap. He taught her to drive, but first
on a tractor! Whenever she had something on her mind or

something had happened at school that upset her, the two of them would meet on the steps of the stoop outside our "nest," which was our small study on the west side of the house. Sitting side-by-side on the steps, Bill would always ask Mary Nelle, "Do you want to start or do you want me to?" He would always listen to what was on her mind, let her vent the emotions that were bothering her, and then help her analyze the situation logically. He focused on helping Mary Nelle realize that she did not have to do what the other kids did. His quiet and gentle guidance helped her learn to make her own choices and be her own person, regardless of what others do or say.

Dear Reader:

This is as far as my mom got in writing about my father, yet there was so much more to say, to share, to record. Perhaps it was all too dear for her to express or perhaps her memories were too many to recount. Perhaps it was because the loss of him twenty years earlier remained too raw or because, in her nineties, she was simply tired.

For whatever reason, this is where her handwritten account of her life with Daddy stopped and without the fitting conclusion she usually crafted for her stories. I know that, as the sensitive teacher she was, she would want this story to feel complete for her readers so I've penned a few thoughts about my dad and shared comments I made at the dedication of the chimes given in his memory to Clopton United Methodist Church. Those thoughts appear in Part Six, A Few Final Words.

~~~M.NMcL

Part Six
A Few Final Words

WB, Mary Nelle, and Vivian McLennan, 1985.

What's Left to Say?

I am an only child though not by my parents' choice. When people asked my mom about her family or if she had other children, she would refer to me and wryly reply, "*No others. She's the crop.*" My parents wanted a large family, but when that wasn't possible, they poured all their love and hopes, energy and devotion into parenting me. Every day, they modeled truth and integrity, humor and compassion, faith and connection. Without reservation, they gave me security and unconditional love as they provided opportunities for me to grow and to build my future.

My parents gave me roots, deep and strong. They taught me to love the land, to care about community, and to act to make things better. Their respect for what went before us, their sense of place, and their fidelity to family grounded me; they ground me still.

Memmie and Daddy also gave me wings and encouraged me to fly. They led me to opportunities, whether it was through all those times my dad sat with me on the front steps and gently helped me find my own voice, or the many late nights and early mornings that my mom took time from her life to shepherd me into mine. And, like that first trip to 4-H camp, those opportunities made all the difference in the paths of my life. These two people helped me believe in myself and to recognize the differences I can make.

In closing this album of memories, there is so much more that could and should be said about both my mom, with all her spunk and generosity, and my hard-working dad, who loved us and shared our lives. The next two pieces are tributes I wrote to honor them at the end of their lives. In 2005, I offered remarks at the dedication of chimes donated to Clopton United Methodist Church in honor of my father, and in 2015, I wrote and delivered the eulogy at my mother's funeral. Those words are my sincere attempt to express my love, respect, and gratitude to my parents.

Like everyone else, Memmie and Daddy were far from perfect, yet melded within their imperfections lay their humanity, their strengths, their authenticity, their love.

They were simply wonderful, and I can never thank them enough.

~~~MNMcL

Remembering
Winfield Brown McLennan

Dedication of Memorial Chimes
Clopton United Methodist Church
October 9, 2005
Authored and delivered by Mary Nelle McLennan

The poet Gibran wrote that, *"Remembrance is a form of meeting."*

When we *remember* those who are far away or gone beyond our world, we *meet* them again with our *spirits*.

My dad, Winfield McLennan, has been gone from this world for eleven years now, but he has never been absent from our hearts or from the living of our lives. My mom commented recently, that each time she hears the bells, it triggers memories of him, bringing back moments long-buried, but not gone. For her, the bells have sparked remembrances of my dad—and have given her a form of meeting him again.

Perhaps these chimes, which we dedicate today, can perform a similar marvel for each person who hears them. Each time we hear the bells, may our minds embrace memories of those we love, of times made dear by moments of grace, of choices and chances that have made us who we are and better yet, who we still *can* be.

Daddy was born in this community and lived his entire life here. He loved it here. It was home. His roots in Clopton ran deep, both in this community and in this church. In the 1830s, the McLennans, his paternal great-grandparents who were immigrants from Scotland, arrived in this community from North Carolina. They carved out a settlement on the land where daddy was born, just three miles west of here. The McLennans joined other early local families in establishing a Methodist circuit in Clopton and laid the foundations for our church today.

His mother's family, the Poindexters, came to this community later in the 1800s. They lived and worked here and worshiped in this church as well. My father's roots and connections in this church are evident in the beautiful windows that surround us—all of them given in memory of folks he knew—some given in memory of his parents, aunts, uncles, and cousins.

My dad was a Scotsman by birth and by nature. He could seem a quiet man, but he was really quite a talker. He could seem a serious man, but he was actually a scamp and a gentle joker.

He could seem a simple man, but he was brilliant and talented, able to build anything, to fix everything, and to give up on nothing. He could seem stubborn. WELL,.....he *was stubborn*!

He loved animals, especially the parade of dogs he nurtured through his lifetime. He hated cruelty of any kind and acted to stop it.

He loved the land he came from and treated it with respect. He was a problem-solver, a true Scotsman, and a marvelous father.

He recognized the power of the past, and he believed in the possibilities of the future.

My dad was my mom's high school boyfriend who became her best friend and life's companion. In fact, sixty-four years ago today, he became her husband as they were married in her family's home in Brighton.

He was a loyal and respected member of Clopton's Methodist Church for his entire life, serving it in many capacities. He was born into this church as was his father before him and his parents before him. My father was baptized here. He worshiped here. He was eulogized here and is buried in this cemetery.

As is natural, the remnants of the early families who established this church are dwindling in number—the Grays and the Whitleys; the Rhodes and the Wrights; the Roanes and the Sigmans; the Kyles and the Morgans and the Anthonys. The McLennans and the Poindexters. Their numbers have grown smaller, but their influence is abundant and alive.

The poet Robinson Jeffers wrote: "Give me the stone strength of the past, and I will give you the wings of the future." So it is with those early families and the foundations they gave us to build on.

So many have given us their stone strength and our own wings for the future. We each have our own memories and those we memorialize for their gifts to us. Too many to name. Too remarkable to be forgotten.

As descendants of one of those original families of this church, my mom and I have chosen to present these chimes in my dad's memory to help link the generations for whom this church has been a gathering place, a foundation, a sanctuary.

We hope the music of these chimes will help us all remember those souls who lived here, worked here, worshiped here, and will always be part of our community's caravan of faith and life.

We hope these chimes will inspire us to move forward, carrying with us their stone strength from the past and the power of the future.

Yes, Winfield Brown McLennan, a loyal son of this fair place, was a good man. I am honored to be his daughter.

Winfield Brown McLennan, 1941.

Remembering Mem

Eulogy for Vivian Baird McLennan
Clopton United Methodist Church
March 8, 2015
Authored and delivered by Mary Nelle McLennan

I thought I knew my mother, and I thought I knew her well. After all, I was the only child she and my dad were able to have, and they selflessly showered their love, time, and attention on me for my entire life. After Rick and I took my mom to Pittsburgh so we could care for her, I had been in her presence nearly every day the last four years, so I thought I knew her well.

I have always known my mother's unconditional love for my dad, for me, and for our family. I have always felt the energy of her vibrant embrace of life and of the lives around her. As a child, I grew to recognize her uncommon commitment to helping others and to serving God's world.

I had no choice but to know, and eventually adopt, her love of everything old and her understanding of what the past means to the future. I still find funny little notes that she taped to the backs of *everything*—notes that say: "This bed was a wedding gift to your great-grandparents Lucretia McCalla and Robert Baird." Or, "The last time this clock ticked was the hour that your great-grandfather Daniel

McLennan died." She made sure I know and love family and family things.

I watched and learned as my mother tirelessly dreamed up, organized, and built creative and cutting-edge lessons and activities for her students, whom she loved. My commitment to serve was kindled by her perennial service to the people of our community and to Clopton Methodist in her many roles as Sunday School teacher, Church officer, MYF Counselor, ice cream supper organizer, cook and bottle washer, and all-around faithful member.

As a young adult making my own way in the world, I was instructed by her fierce independence. Through my middle years, she stood by me and with me through celebrations of triumphs and through the pain of wrenching heartbreaks. I was inspired by her courage as my mother reshaped her life after my dad's death twenty-one years ago this month.

I was amazed by Memmie's spunk as she continued to care for and tinker on the home she and my daddy had built on McLennan Road. Greg Scott was recently laughing about the times she hired him to help her with work around the place. What really happened, he explained, is that she would have him hold the ladder while she drove the nails!

I was awed by her grace as she aged and dealt with vision loss, a broken hip and two fractured arms, and fading memory. And I will always be touched by her endearing charm as she regretfully gave up her independence and learned to depend on and cultivate the love of her caregivers in assisted living and skilled care settings.

I thought I knew my mother, but over these past few days—
through conversations, calls, and comments by many of you
and countless others—I have learned of rich and significant
insights into who she truly was, and of her quiet—and
sometimes *not* so quiet—often-impish, always-sincere zest for
life.

My family and I have heard of her impact as a matriarch,
valued friend, mentor, inspiration, fun-loving side-kick,
remarkable teacher, talented leader, and a worker willing to
roll up her sleeves. Thank you for sharing your memories
and stories of how she touched your lives.

I have learned that, by her example and by her direction, she
taught us important LIFE LESSONS:

She taught us that all life is scared:

> If she were driving along and spied a turtle in the
> road, she would pull over—and sometimes stop
> traffic—pick up the turtle and put him in the weeds
> on the side of the road to which he was headed. She
> always taught me that you take him in the direction
> he was going. Never in the direction he came from,
> even if that was easier…. What a metaphor for her
> approach to teaching and to life!

She taught us to support the little guy.

> If she needed her car washed, Mem would find a car
> wash being held by kids from a school or church or
> club. She would say that it would cost more, and they

> would not do as good a job, *but* that it would help
> make a difference. And if she had a choice of gas
> stations or stores to shop, she would choose the
> smaller, independent or even one that appeared run-
> down because she wanted to support "the little guy."

She taught us that small, generous acts can change a life.

> Using her own car and gasoline, for years, my mom
> ran the unofficial Clopton Methodist Sunday School
> shuttle. She drove all around the community and
> beyond, picking up and returning home children
> whose families did not come to church. She picked
> them up for Sunday School and MYF. It did not
> matter how far or what the weather, she was there to
> get them and to take them home—and she made it
> fun.

A couple of days ago, I received a call from my cousin,
Carol Ann Poindexter Williams, who grew up in this
community and this church. Carol Ann called to give her
sympathy, but more importantly, she went on to say that
recently she was asked to speak about a person who had
influenced her life. She chose my mom, saying that "Miss
Vivian" had given her opportunities and experiences she
would never have known without my mom's silent generosity.
Carol Ann explained that my mom, quietly and without
notice, made sure she did not miss out on activities she
would not have been able to afford. And my cousin
emphasized that those opportunities changed her life in
remarkable and lasting ways.

Yesterday, John Earl Wells was remembering that long before federal programs offered financial and medical support for people in need, my mom and dad quietly took needy children to eye doctors, dentists, orthodontists, and clothing stores where they personally paid for the children's glasses, dental work, and warm clothing. They really lived the scripture: "Unto the least of these."

My mom truly taught us that small, generous acts can change lives.

Perhaps Mem's most powerful lesson was that *each person counts and that learning can change a life.*

My mom loved the John Adams quote, "Let us dare to read, think, speak, and write." She kept that quote tucked inside her billfold most of her years. If someone mentioned that she was a "school teacher," she quickly, but politely corrected that concept by saying, "I don't teach school. *I teach children.*"

Long before the development of the theory and research on "transformational education," she *was* a transformational teacher. As Courtney Fee said yesterday, "Vivian could have written the book on it!" She laid a firm foundation for the best in education today.

My mother taught her students not only their traditional "book learning" lessons, but also about themselves, about life, about living in meaningful ways, and about giving to others and society.

As a young teacher right out of Memphis State Teachers' College, now the University of Memphis, she began her teaching career in a combined third and fourth grade classroom in Burlison's eight-grade, four-teacher school during the depression. Those students she lovingly called her "children," became her life-long "groupies." For decades, they took her to lunch once a month just to be together. She was, and even after her death, has remained a transformative teacher whose impact has gone far beyond her classroom. She prepared her students for far more than their next grade and helped them discover life-lessons that served them throughout their adulthood. Both intentionally and unintentionally, she taught others how to teach.

One of her students said to me, "She took us under her wings….and then she gave us our own wings." Miss Vivian's lasting impact on her students is best expressed in some of their own words. I am sharing two letters: one from a student in her first class at Burlison; another from a student she taught many years later in the Brighton School.

First, a letter from one of her very first students:

Dear Mary Nelle,

I'm writing to let you know I'm sorry to hear of your mother's passing, and to tell you I won't be able to be at her funeral.

She came to Burlison School in the late Thirties to teach 4th grade. Everyone at school loved her. She was a bright and shining light in the depression years of the Thirties. I remember well how the room and the day took on new meaning when she came every morning driving a 1937 Ford, black and shining.

Burlison and 4th grade was her first job and her first love. When she taught at Burlison the County had no money. They paid her with an IOU. She took the job at $45 a month.

She had to quit teaching when she got married to your Dad because of a County or State law. In later years she taught at Brighton.

In the late Eighties or early Nineties, Miss Vivian wanted to have a Burlison Reunion for her 4th grade class and we did. We had a good turnout. After we had lunch, we talked and told stories and had fun. Miss Vivian surprised us by bringing her roll-call book from 1938 or 1939. When she called our name, we had to stand up and be counted.

Miss Vivian always called us her children. She loved us like a teacher and a mother, and we all loved her. Everyone at school knew her, and she knew everyone and had time to help them if they needed it.

I never had another teacher like her. She ruled with love, not a paddle. I'm thankful for all the years I knew her.

A Friend with Love,
M.B. Walker

And, a journal entry from one of her later students, Nora Smith Krainis, now a teacher in Maine:

January 23, 2013
Today Miss Vivian is 96 years old.
Miss Vivian was my fourth-grade teacher. Because of
Miss Vivian –

I don't write a card without making sure I leave room
to write a nicely placed complimentary close and
signature line.

I make sure I have enough room on a line to finish the
line, or I start a new one. I don't tuck the words under the
end of the line.

I don't say "O" when referring to a number. I say
"zero." ("Now, Nora Belle, you know the number is
'zero;' it is not a letter.')

I very carefully write the address in the center of the
envelope and along a straight left margin.

I don't pick up an iron without thinking about the
people who lived during the frontier days using those
heavy coal irons. The same goes for curling irons. I
always think about the irons they would put in the lamps
to heat up. (Mrs. Vivian curled my hair with one of those
for Frontier Days.)

If there is a student who has talent, I figure out a way
to let that talent shine.

Because of Miss Vivian, I'm in love with costumes.

I love buttons made of shells, and vividly remember
her sample of a shell that had holes in it from buttons
being cut out of it.

I have high expectations of students and help them reach those expectations.

I teach students to take pride in their work.

I call the students what they want to be called.

I "get into" the students' world and try to see it as they do.

I try to make students think outside the box.

I stay in touch with those special ones with whom I've connected, and with their families, hoping I have or will make a difference in their lives like Miss Vivian did in mine.

I take time to talk to students who come back to visit and to their parents when I see them in town.

Because of Miss Vivian, I am a teacher.

With love from your Nora Belle.

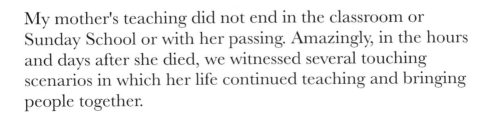

My mother's teaching did not end in the classroom or Sunday School or with her passing. Amazingly, in the hours and days after she died, we witnessed several touching scenarios in which her life continued teaching and bringing people together.

Vivian Baird McLennan, 1941.

Simply put…Vivian Baird McLennan changed lives.

But most important to me, she was my mother…my "Memmie."

She gave me birth—but she *also* gave me *life*. She taught me kindness. She taught me courage. She taught me to give, and to give even when you do not get. She taught me the power of fairness and honesty. She taught me to always, *always* take the high road. But most of all, she taught me love.

She was and will always be a blessing.

I love you, Mem…

Mary Nelle's Closing Thoughts

The kitchen was warm when I walked through to hush the tea kettle's whistle. I could overhear my mom and Rick murmuring through the transcription of one of her recollected stories. It was an afternoon like so many others when those two teamed up to crystalize her memories, yet suddenly something was different—everything was different. I was frozen in place, clutched first by an unbidden chill, then by the unwelcome acknowledgment that these precious moments would too soon happen only in my memory.

In that chilling moment, I recognized what I already knew.

I saw that Mem's desire and commitment to tell her stories of family and community were far stronger than any disability caused by blindness or injury or age. I witnessed her resilience and her commitment to life that had burned brightly through her ninety-eight years of living, the last twenty without her beloved husband, my dad, by her side. I saw her spirit dance.

Still chilled, still frozen, I witnessed *again* Rick's endless capacity for kindness, compassion, humor, and unselfish love, all traits that had driven his entire life's journey. There, in action in front of me, for me to see and hear, was his living commitment to family, to me, and to the task of making the world more gentle, one constant act after another.

And I recognized the richness of these times while realizing that this Camelot could not last.

———————◆———————

My mother died on February 26, 2015, at the age of ninety-eight, only five months after Rick's death in September of 2014. They both leave huge holes in my fabric, but it is a weft made stronger and resilient by their freely given love and unselfishness and character.

While that time we enjoyed is gone, as are my mother and Rick, we have the power of her memories to help us meet and honor people, times, and places that carved the history of a small west Tennessee town in the 1920s and 1930s and into the years to follow. Building these vignettes into a book has been a labor, but also a gift of insight. Mem's memories help us see the potential of our own ordinary days and of regular people. They provide a lens on life that enriches our understanding of the world we inherited. Such stories connect where we have been with where we can go.

With my mom's death went countless other memories and recollections that we were not able to capture, but we are blessed with these sixty-two stories she gave us. Without such recollections, those times and people and places could easily evaporate from our common memory and leave us knowing less of who we actually are.

As this album comes to a close, I carry deep hope that this will not be the close of our looks back at what came before us and what we have been given to make better. Instead, I hope these reflections of past times and people will encourage each of us to ask questions about the lives of our families and neighbors and even those we meet casually, serendipitously.

And I deeply hope that we listen—*really listen*—to the stories they tell us…Stories about the history they helped unfold, which can be inspiration to help us create our own better histories.

~~~ *Mary Nelle McLennan*
2021

</div>

Acknowledgements

Dig Under or Crawl Over is the work of my "Mem" who remembered these stories, shared them for decades in her storytelling way, and, at the end of her life, hand-wrote each one despite the challenges of failing vision. Her gifts as a naturally transformative teacher did not fall fallow when she left the classroom; they were evident the rest of her life, and they are bright and alive in each recollection shared here. I am deeply grateful for her tenacity in documenting these people, places, and times, and for passing on to me a sense of place as well as a sense of belonging.

My late husband and partner in everything, Richard "Rick" Welsh, was a perpetual cheerleader for Mem's efforts to write her stories. For years, the two of them enjoyed a warm friendship and a special connection all their own; their unique relationship, coupled with Rick's generous gifts of time and undivided attention, became a scaffold for her as she labored to refine each story, revising them over and over. Through his characteristic kindness, silly wit, and respect for writing, Rick sheltered her from doubts, and he strengthened her resolve. Just as he always did for me, and as his memory still does, Rick made her better, and he helped her believe.

A troop of talented and faithful collaborators whom I call the "Home Team" helped advance the compilation, editing, and publication of this book. The long-haulers who are recognized below contributed far more than just their work —they invested their spirit.

My deepest debt is to the "wise and spry" *Marie Amerson*, herself a gifted and published writer, who has been my constant support and an incredible resource as the publisher of this work. She adopted this project with a commitment as strong as if it were her own. I'm sure she did so largely because she believes in the power of preserving stories of regular people and places. And perhaps because she is a true friend of thirty-plus years. Without Marie's exceptional talents, her gracious patience, and her amazing ability to design and deploy a complex plan of countless details, I would never have been able to bring these memories to readers. You are holding this book because of her.

It is my great fortune that Marie and her husband, *Jerry Amerson*, are a package deal! Jerry has supported us with his technical and photographic skills as well as his mastery with a red pen. His cool head and wholesome humor have gotten us through more than just a few scrapes. And besides all that, Jerry is a great cook and superlative kitchen help!

Brenda Egan—dear friend, professional colleague, and travel "bestie"—has been my honest-but-gentle proofreader throughout years of editing. She has also been my faithful enforcer, my continual encourager, and my daily reality check. Brenda's unflagging friendship helped me keep this project bubbling after the deaths of Rick and Mem and through the grief-fog of those times. Fortunately, she's done all this despite my fondness of em dashes.

David Gwinn, a local historian and genealogist from Brighton, has been an irreplaceable asset for both my mom and for me. His incredible understanding of Tipton County's past and the intertwining of local families for two centuries is exceeded only by his willingness to dip into his exhaustive repository to fish out illusive information. For years, he kindly fielded frequent calls from Mem as she verified the accuracy of her memories; more recently, he has been a remarkable resource for me. Thank you, David!

Our efforts to publish Mem's stories were reinforced by many encouragers throughout this endeavor. I want to recognize the following individuals for the energy they gave us.

Cousins Annette McCain Feaver, Lynn Baird Griffin, Dianne Feaver Lewis, and Mary Ann McLennan served as validating resources, but more importantly, they cared. Rick's sister, Eileen Quolke, has believed in this and encouraged me, too. These women are my proxy sisters.

Janisse Ray, author and teacher, has been inspirational and instructional. She, along with my fellow writers from our Parker Ranch sessions in the north Georgia mountains, bolstered my belief that these stories hold pieces of life to be honored, and they helped me figure out how to do it. Special acknowledgments to writers Susan, Tom, and Marie.

My former student John Hassler, whom I taught years ago at the Tennessee School for the Blind, has been my relentless nudge, calling at least weekly for two years to ask, "Did you work on *The Book* this week?" Finally getting even with his teacher, perhaps?

Numbers of my mom's former students and fellow teachers, with whom she would serendipitously visit at Covington's McDonald's or Walmart, have encouraged us to take these stories beyond their original bounds. Thanks to each of you for your kindnesses to my mom.

And a final nod goes to the late John Prine whose wry and honest music kept me chuckling through many tedious hours at my laptop.

> *I'm sorry my son, but you're too late in asking;*
> *Mr. Peabody's coal train has hauled it away.*
> ~~~ *John Prine*

Made in the USA
Coppell, TX
16 November 2021

65832813R00192